Discovery-Based Retail

Unlock Your Store's Potential!

Philip H. Mitchell

Bascom Hill Publishing Group
212 3rd Avenue North, Suite 570
Minneapolis, MN 55401
612-455-2293
www.bascomhillpublishing.com

ISBN - 0-9798467-9-x
ISBN - 978-0-9798467-9-3
LCCN - 2008924098

Book sales for North America and international:
Itasca Books, 3501 Highway 100 South, Suite220
Minneapolis, MN 55416
Phone: 952.345.4488 (toll free 1.800.901.3480)
Fax: 952.920.0541; email to orders@itascabooks.com

Cover Design by Jenni Wheeler
Typeset by Peggy LeTrent

"I feel that, without question, Phil Mitchell's Discovery-Based Retail *covers all the key elements better than any publication I have read. Phil's focus on change in the marketplace, customer service and identifying your business type is clearly defined along with product assortment, advertising and merchandising.* Discovery-Based Retail *is indeed a worthwhile read for anyone involved in retailing."*

—Joe Thomlinson — Retired, Valspar Corporation

"Discovery-Based Retail is ... something that could be of great help to anyone in the retail lumber and building material business/hardware business."

—Mike Kennedy, President/CEO, T.H. Rogers Lumber Company, Edmond, Oklahoma

"For the past 15 years, my job at the North American Retail Hardware Association has been generating editorial and training content designed to help make independent home-improvement retailers better and more profitable merchants. During that time, I have yet to read a book that addresses so many of the issues that specifically affect a home-improvement retailer's success as well as Phil Mitchell does in Discovery-Based Retail. *It should be required reading for retailers in any industry, but especially for home-improvement retailers.*

I first met Mitchell during an interview. I was the writer and he was the interview subject. He had just been appointed vice president of sales for an industry wholesaler. But, shortly into the interview, it became clear that he was much more than your typical industry executive. Phil is a student of retailing — someone who has spent his entire career helping retailers achieve greater levels of success and inspiring them to change.

Inspiring change is what this book is about. It touches on each of the critical variables that retailers need to address: customer service issues, assortment planning, employee training, pricing/margin strategies, how customers shop and especially store layout and design. Just like retailing, this book is part art and part science. It's part history lesson and part road map, designed to help you reveal your own unique path to retail success."

—Scott Wright, North American Retail Hardware Association

To Jack Laurie, a great friend who taught me much, made me laugh, and left this world way too soon!

Table of Contents

Foreword

It has been said that the days of gaining a competitive advantage with product or price are dead, a rather sobering thought but one that's hard to argue, too. Our company, Home Lumber & Supply Co., has been in business since 1905, and we've seen more change in the retail environment in the last 25 years than in the previous 75-plus. We've experienced and survived the "How can we ever compete against that?" mentality with a generation of enthusiastic, aggressive store managers who are service oriented and community minded. Ours are *the* HOME-town teams in the county seats of rural southern Kansas. Sales growth, in and of itself, is pretty exciting stuff in slower growth markets like those our stores inhabit, but as we all know, there's much more to maintaining a desired level of profitability than just sales growth.

My first encounter with Phil Mitchell was a cold call four years ago at one of our stores that did not buy hardware from the firm he represented as a regional sales manager. We were relocating the store, and I was working with the current hardware supplier on a new floor plan and décor package. I was disappointed with what they were proposing, and Phil seized the moment (he doesn't miss many opportunities like that) to share one of his recent plans for a similar-sized store in another state. Although I am not a professional store designer, I can recognize an efficient use of space, a comfortable environment, and a fresh look that offers potential to get people — employees and customers — excited about a change. Phil's design showed imagination with a sharp focus on our building and community needs. My first encounter with

Phil was the start of a very important relationship to me both personally and professionally.

There is a side to Phil that helps explain his unique approach to the retail or management business: He is a talented musician, voracious reader, storyteller, pilot of experimental craft, and a thoughtful writer. Store design is indeed "part science and part art," and Phil possesses special personal qualities that can take projects and processes to a higher level. I can't tell you how many times he's used "But imagine if you will ..." on me, but that creative engagement with space and retail processes will become quite evident as you read *Discovery-Based Retail*.

Phil has true passion for organizational management — more than anyone I've known in 30-plus years in the industry. He can step into your retailer's shoes and then into your customers' shoes in the blink of an eye, and then prioritize the plethora of action items needed to improve a store based on these perspectives. He's got a folksy, comfortable way of reminding us of the common sense basics. His liberal use of metaphors and analogies helps define some revolutionary new concepts in everyday language. "Space and inventory enhancement" could be overly technical, but when you add an interactive calculator to automatically determine your options, the concept becomes functional, an easy-to-use tool that can improve your store's profitability. Phil has helped us "plow straighter rows," and we are becoming a better company because of it.

Since our first project together, we have thrown Phil, the consultant, several curveballs; our individual stores, communities, and personalities are as different as night and day. I wondered at the outset if he could embrace the differences or if he would, like others before him, try to blend them completely into a one-size-fits-all option. To my delight, Phil successfully managed the former. As he repeatedly points out in the book, the basic retail principles are the same from one retail situation to the next, but the means to achieving higher profitability goals are constantly changing from market to market. Now more than ever before, retailers must be proactive, watching our market and our competitors, and then rebuilding our stores around our target customers.

Productivity improvement requires a sharp focus, which can sometimes elude those of us on the inside looking out. We've tried the perspective of an "outsider" from time to time — some have been helpful and others an embarrassing waste of resources. *Discovery-Based Retail* is a resource worth reading and utilizing. You will enjoy getting acquainted with Phil Mitchell while being challenged with cutting-edge concepts.

John Humphreys
General Manager
Home Lumber and Supply Company
Ashland, Kansas

Introduction

Whether you have been in business for a short time or for many years, it is a safe bet that you have a sense of the changing retail environment within which your store operates. In communities where there were once many thriving businesses, there are now only a handful. Colossal mega-stores are now in small communities where, heretofore, it would have seemed unlikely that such small towns possessed the demographics to attract these behemoths. If history tells us anything, it is that these giant mega-stores will also evolve into something new and different in their turn. As Bob Dylan so eloquently sang many years ago, "For the times they are a-changin'." In short, there have always been changes in the retail business sector and there always will be, but the way your business changes and the way it evolves will determine whether it survives — let alone whether it thrives.

As you read through this book you will learn that my experiences have been in the variety, hardware, and home center sectors. Don't let this fact or my antecdotes and references to these store types disuade you from reading further if your retail offering is different. The fundamental applications will stand up from category to category and the lessons learned will be sound.

I find it all mind-boggling. Perhaps it's just the perspective of someone in his mid-50s, who has devoted a lifetime to the same industry, but it seems to me that the evolution of the hardware retailing business is an enigma. On the one hand, there have been profound changes. There are fewer stores and fewer suppliers. In fact, perhaps in no other industry is the phrase "survival of the fittest" more apropos. Faced with changing trends and changing demographics, many wholesalers and retailers alike have been rendered noncompetitive and ultimately insolvent. On the other hand, however, the basics of the retail process — acquiring merchandise, assigning a markup, and then selling that merchandise — have remained virtually unchanged.

It's important to have an understanding of what caused some of the major changes, how these changes have affected our industry, and how circumstances in the hardware industry are likely to continue to evolve.

In 1744, Captain John Ames decided that he could produce metal shovels in colonial America that were as good or better than anything being made in England. Many historians point to this event as the birth of the hardware industry in America. Ironically, given all of the changes in the hardware industry in recent years, the Ames Tool Company is still in business today and is the oldest brand in America. The Ames Company (now Ames True Temper) has apparently evolved to stay ahead of the curve of changing trends and changing times.

There is a lesson that all of us in retail should learn from companies that have stood the test of time: Good companies continue to evolve! And although you, as a storeowner or manager, may be resistant to change, you must be fully cognizant that change is a certain part of your store's future. In fact, without change, your store does not have a long-term future!

For 200 years following Ames's introduction of his steel shovel line, the hardware industry remained basically static. Manufacturing methodology evolved, of course, and distribution channels changed, but the retail process itself stayed fundamentally the same. There was a hardware store in every small town, and sometimes multiple stores in towns of as few as 500 to 600 people. Mobility was limited, product awareness was limited, and information was passed primarily by word of mouth. Aaron Montgomery Ward founded his mail order business in 1872 and elevated awareness of new products, but the product offering of retail hardware stores stayed relatively consistent.

Contrast that environment with the one in which a retailer must operate today. A viable hardware store in a community of 500 to 600 people is becoming increasingly rare. It is simply a matter of economics. A shrinking rural demographic, smaller profit margins, and higher expenses have destroyed all but the shrewdest operators in these mini-markets.

Products are introduced and touted on the World Wide Web, on every television set, and in every magazine in America. We live in an "incredible shrinking world" in which, with the click of a computer mouse, one can access an almost limitless amount of information from around the world, and do so without leaving the comfort of one's own home. Is it any wonder, then, that shoppers are more aware of price and more demanding of selection? After all, with another click they can even order the products that they peruse and have them shipped to their front door, acquiring these products without ever having set foot in a retail store.

At first consideration, it might seem that all "walk-in" retail is doomed, but such is not the case. There are three very important factors that are not addressed in the impersonal model of online shopping.

We are not, as a species, patient and so the number one factor in walk-in retail's advantage is the desire for instant gratification. Simply put, if a person has a need for an item and can take delivery when that need is the greatest, he or she will gravitate to the local, and immediately available, source. If the local merchant has an item in stock, that merchant obviously has the advantage.

The second factor in the survival of walk-in retailers is the fact that we like to touch the things we are going to buy. For example, something as basic as a hammer is usually weight-and-balance tested in a retail store by a prospective consumer. This simple action is obviously not possible with an Internet offering, and this is another winning point for the local retailer.

And finally, although occasionally interaction with other people might seem undesirable, the ability to ask questions and have them answered face to face — to be called by name and recognized as a regular customer — will be difficult to replace in any virtual medium. Simply put, humans desire personal communication and recognition, and the walk-in retailer offers these elements to the purchaser of goods.

Another phenomenon that faces merchants today is that we no longer live and work in a circumscribed space. As mobility has increased, the world has literally gotten smaller. In the 50s, when I was a child, a weekly trip to a neighboring town of 5,000 people was an event and, at least in my rural community, a trip to the city was a vacation, a once a year getaway. Presently, people have no qualms about driving a hundred miles to shop for everyday items, which has an impact on local retailers of the area from which those consumers depart.

Given this new climate of mobility, it is perhaps ironic that planners still utilize a retail axiom and formula originally penned in 1931 to show the likely division between two trade centers at which shoppers will go one way or the other. William J. Reilly first put forth his theory in a book entitled *Reilly's Law of Retail Gravitation.* The formula goes like this:

$$Bp = \frac{d}{(1+(\sqrt{(p1/p2)})}$$

According to Wikipedia, the formula means: "the balance or Break Point (*BP*) is equal to the Distance (*d*) between two places, divided by the following: Unity or Total (1) plus the Square Root of, the size of Place One (*p1*) divided by the size of Place Two (*p2*)."(1)

Using this formula, boundaries of a trade territory can be established that accurately show retail potential within a given area.

His formula was inspired by Isaac Newton's Law of Gravitation, in which Newton stated that "two bodies attract each other with a force that is proportional to the product of their masses and inversely proportional to the square of the distance between them."

Perhaps Reilly's formula is not important to you, but it is important to remember that people are attracted to larger cities and larger retail stores with broader product offerings. To continue Reilly's analogy to gravity, it is interesting to observe that, although it requires a great deal of energy, we can escape the gravitational pull of the earth itself — our space shuttles do it all the time. It takes a tremendous amount of effort, but we do it. Likewise, sometimes customers escape the retail gravitational pull that Reilly described, but it requires a great amount of resources from the winning trade center or individual retailer, usually in the form of advertising and aggressive pricing.

Of course, our discussion would not be complete without taking a look at the differences in historical and current hardware pricing; of any trend, changes in retail pricing have probably had the biggest impact on local merchants.

Until the late 1960s, pricing was usually done by "keystoning," a pricing methodology that relied on taking the cost of an item and doubling it to establish the retail price. When an item sold, it generated a 50 percent margin, meaning that ½ of the retail price was cost and the other half was margin or profit.

That was all well and good when everybody was doing it, but with the entrance of discounters into the marketplace, including Wal-Mart stores in 1962, everything changed. Discounters began to use a variable pricing system that would even include "loss leaders," (advertised items that were sacrificed below cost) in order to lure customers into a store. This "variable pricing" structure had two distinct advantages: it could help establish a better pricing image and thus improve sales, and by taking some prices even higher than the keystone method, could actually improve overall margins in some cases. Retailers who continued to price their products using the old keystone system began to look silly or, worse yet, greedy in this new culture.

Today, a dynamic and comprehensive pricing structure is a must! Many wholesalers offer sophisticated systems to help a store develop a price-competitive image while assuring that storewide margins remain adequate, which is necessary in today's retail climate just as it's always been. However, it is of grave concern that retailers often rely on their wholesaler for the development of their pricing system. Their pricing system has a huge impact on their store's success, but the store manager assumes that his wholesaler has done all of the necessary legwork. In truth, no wholesale company's system adequately addresses the dynamics of individual retailers' operations. You will learn more about this later in the book.

My first entry into the lumber and hardware business was in 1970 at the O.E. Woods Lumber Company in Ft. Scott, Kansas. I tried to be the best deliveryman that small store had ever employed. I don't know if I succeeded in that regard, but I do know that I learned a lot from Ed, the old gentleman who was an owner-partner, the operating manager, and my boss. Sometimes I was a willing student and sometimes I wasn't, but his messages were always firm and, in retrospect, always spot-on.

For example, there was the day — about noon on a Saturday, which was quitting time — when he told me to sweep around the nail bins. I was sweeping up the nails that had fallen on the floor. My plan was to pick up the nails and trash them, my motto, or perhaps excuse, being that cleanliness is next to godliness and all that. But Ed noticed what I was doing and intervened just in time.

"Sort those nails and put them back in the bins," he said.

"Gosh Ed, there aren't 15 cents-worth of nails here," I replied in my own defense.

"Son, remember this," he said. "If you take care of the little things, the big things will take care of themselves!"

I did remember that lesson, and although his point might have seemed extreme that day, at some point in my career, his words resonated with me. In fact, I have worked in the lumber and hardware industry since that time, and I have had the opportunity to learn many lessons from some great teachers, but none has been more important than the one Ed taught me that day. Ed's message is just as valid today as it was 36 years ago.

As I said, there were many other lessons, however. For example, there was the lesson I learned from Richard. During my yearlong management-training period with the TG&Y Company, an early-day discount variety store chain, I set up an end-cap display. I don't remember the product, but I do remember that it wasn't breakable, and as it turned out, that was a good thing. Richard walked up to the display and, with one swoop of his gigantic arm, swept all of the products in the display to the floor. He then turned to me and said, "Do it again now, and don't leave so much space between the shelves. People will think that we bought more if the end cap looks nice and full. They will think they're getting a better deal, and if they think they're getting a better deal, they'll buy more."

Was he right? Yeah, probably so. Store #1407 was one of the most successful stores in the Tulsa division.

The constant tutelage that I benefited from *should be* even more important to retailers today than it was then. The retail environment, after all, is more competitive than ever. However, ongoing training and mentoring is being lost to the pressures of cutting costs. There is a continued and constant bottom-line examination of expenses, as there should be, but because the benefits incurred from providing additional training are sometimes difficult to quantify, this part of a budget (if it is budgeted at all) is often the first to be axed.

It is true that the benefits of ongoing training *are* difficult to quantify, but a "cutback mentality" takes a shortsighted view of today's problems and offers at best a blurred vision of long-term opportunities. Employees should be any business's greatest asset, but when the burden of development falls upon owners, management, and supervisors with no time, there is often no training at all.

The wholesale hardware company where I worked for 23 years provided occasional outside training. Some of the training was top-notch and some wasn't, but all of the training was beneficial because it provided us with outside opinions of retail processes and, therefore, new perspectives, widening our knowledge base. As the cliché goes, knowledge is power, and in retail, as is the case for most other human endeavors, power is a good thing.

When the orange and blue mega-box-stores first came onto the scene, rocking the lumber and hardware industry, the employees at smaller stores, many with very long and illustrious retail histories, were told, "We can out-service them — people will come to us for what we know." Well, it's time to wake up and smell the coffee. Those mega-stores have liberal budgets for ongoing employee training, and they shout this fact not only to their customers but to yours. Ask yourself this question: What ongoing training does your store have in place and how do you let consumers know about it? The answer should probably scare you.

As I worked my way up from sales trainee to territory manager, from regional sales manager to Vice President of Sales for that hardware wholesaler, I had the opportunity to work with many store managers.

Please don't take this wrong, but I became convinced that some of these stores survived not because of their strategies but in spite of them.

How is this possible? Simply put, many storeowners possess strong entrepreneurial spirits but lack sufficient information and, perhaps, the time to gather the pertinent information, to operate their business from a truly *informed* perspective. These people are blessed with strength of spirit and drive, and assume that they will overcome anything that they might encounter, which they often do. However, operating a retail business without access to all the information available is not management by action, but rather reactive "survivalism."

Even those managers who have gathered sufficient working knowledge to handle the day-to-day operation of their stores often get caught up in the old "can't see the forest for the trees" syndrome. As one manager told me after my consulting visit, "Phil, I guess I had looked at it for so long that I just couldn't see it"

He isn't alone, not by any means! Owners and managers make their daily pilgrimages through the front doors of their stores or, even worse, through the back doors, with a thousand things on their minds. Discerning how their stores appeal to customers and prospective customers (or how they don't) is probably not on their priority list on a daily basis, but it should be!

This book is all about discovering new elements of your retail business that you might overlook, or look right through, as you go about your everyday responsibilities. The book is also about discovering new ideas, and as the title *Discovery-Based Retail* implies it is about making decisions based upon what can be learned through the Discovery Process.

I am quite sure that if I placed a puzzle before you, made sure that you had all of the pieces, and showed you how the final picture should look, you could put the puzzle together given sufficient time. If, however, you did not have all of the pieces, there would be no way that the assembly could take place. Even if you had all of the pieces but didn't know what the picture was supposed to look like before you started, the assembly process would be, at best, much more time consuming and, at worst, a failure.

Your business *is* much like a puzzle. So, even if you have a mental image of what you would like your business to become, have you gathered all the pieces necessary to assemble it? Perhaps you know the answers, but are you asking the right questions?

Here are some of the right questions: Who are your customers? Where do they come from? How did they become aware of you? Do they think your products are priced competitively? Do your customers feel confident that they will find what they want when they come to your store? How do your customers move through your store? Does the direction of their travel decrease their shopping time or make them less likely to shop one section of the store than another? Is the lighting better in one section of the store than another, and does that impact your sales per square foot accordingly? How do the dollars of inventory per square foot correlate with sales per square foot when departments are compared? Do your employees exceed your customer's expectations? How does your store fit into the arena in which it operates, and how does that positioning guide your daily efforts?

We will talk about a Discovery Process that will help you answer these questions. If you choose to go through the processes outlined in this book, you will assemble the pieces necessary to solve the puzzle that is your business. You will then be able to manage your store from a power position. Again, knowledge is power, and this book is about accumulating knowledge that can guide you through processes that will improve your profitability.

Yes, Bobby Dylan, the times they are a-changin', but these changes need not spell the end of local retail. Quite the contrary, our current retail environment is a showcase for opportunity. Those merchants who maintain a "can do" attitude and a "do" action plan will not only survive but many will even thrive.

If you read through this book and are convinced that the processes are valid but you do not have sufficient staffing to undertake them, someone from our team will be happy to talk to you about our company and how we can complete the process for you. Either way, get started! Either way, get excited! The future of your business is at hand!

Admittedly, I would bet that Columbus felt a myriad of emotions when he set out on his discovery odyssey, and you will, too. Columbus was probably excited, but I'll wager that his excitement was tempered with concern and fear of the unknown. Your Discovery Process may well include fear of the unknown too, but I suggest you let, as I am sure Columbus did, the singular feeling of anticipatory excitement be your guide. You are about to begin a journey that can propel your business to new levels. Once you begin learning new and key information about your business and your competitors your store can meet and, perhaps even exceed, your expectations.

After each chapter, I have highlighted key points and action steps that can help you start the processes. I suggest you share the key points with your staff and begin making plans for implementing your Discovery Process.

Let's set sail then! Let's get started! You're in for some exciting new discoveries, and if you complete the journey, you will return with information that will serve as a map to the treasures of improved profitability.

Points to Remember

1. Change is a constant in both life and the retail environment in which your store operates.
2. Local retail is here to stay!
3. The "shrinking world" phenomenon dictates that a store manager must operate at a higher level of execution than in the past.

Action Steps

1. Prepare your mind to entertain the possibility of change.
2. Encourage your key personnel to read *Discovery-Based Retail* at the same time you are, so that you may compare notes and immediately implement changes as opportunities reveal themselves.

CHAPTER 1

DISCOVERING: THE PROCESS

The Discovery Process is a systematic way of looking at every aspect of your business with the eyes of an objective outsider. It is a series of procedures, exercises and thought processes to guide you through making your store more appealling to your customers. The system also includes spreadsheets and analytical methods to improve your store's profitability and to help you focus on the future. Although, in this book, I apply it to hardware stores and home centers, it is a beneficial process for any retailer, from a dollar store to a craft store, from an auto parts store to the grocery business. Discovery is simply uncovering those nuggets of truth that have, for too long, been hidden within your business. The process involves asking questions, a lot of questions. It involves research and looking at things in a new way.

One of my favorite writers, Wayne Dyer, says it like this: "When you change the way you look at things, the things you look at change." This may sound like just a clever play on words, but I believe this assertion is a fundamental truth. And when it comes to retail operations, changing the way you look at things opens up great new possibilities.

I mentioned that the process demands objectivity. Perhaps this is the most difficult challenge you will face. As an aside, I am a certified trainer for a time management and organizational procedure called the GO System. Developed by Chris Crouch of Memphis, Tennessee, the GO system is a comprehensive approach to developing the organizational and time management skills that elude too many of us. I often start my presentation with the story of pulling up in front of a lumberyard and hearing a blood-curdling scream from the area that I believed to be the saw room. I ran to the saw room to find my worst fears realized: the table of an old Dewalt radial arm saw covered with blood. The side of the saw operator's head was also covered in blood, and this man was on all fours looking for his ear, which he explained he had just sawed off while examining his cut line too closely. I joined the injured man on the floor, and after a little bit of sifting through the sawdust, I found his ear and passed it to him. He took it and examined it closely while rotating it to every possible position.

"This isn't my ear," he eventually proclaimed. "It can't be! My ear had a pencil behind it."

The class usually gets a good laugh out of the story, but what is not so funny is the fact that, just like this man who didn't even recognize his own ear, we sometimes have trouble taking an objective look at our businesses and ourselves. As you read, I suggest trying to shed the rose-colored glasses — be open and be critical as you examine your store through what will be, in effect, new eyes. If you can accomplish this one thing, it will be worth the price you paid for this book!

We will start with a process that examines your customers. Who are they? How can you best serve their needs and desires?

Once we have established who your customers are, we will move on and examine how to maximize your sales opportunities with them. You will learn how the knowledge of who your customers are can help you with decisions from product assortment to advertising and from product display to lighting considerations.

You will learn a process called PDQ that will help you determine how people move through your store. It will pinpoint areas of opportunity regarding your store's sales floor layout. After you have learned to recognize the weaknesses discovered through this process, the following chapter will cover design concepts for improved performance.

The Discovery Process includes an exercise to help you focus on your store's lighting. With an aging population, this is a critical consideration that is becoming more important. You'll learn why. That chapter will also include a discussion about proper signage for your store's peak performance.

Chapter 7 will shake up your preconceived notions of the question: what is customer service?. You will never define that critical area of your store's success the same again!

The Discovery Process is comprehensive and in addition to the things I've already mentioned includes discussions and systems to address advertising, competitive analysis, space and inventory enhancement, retail pricing and how your store fits into the community.

In his book *Category Killers*, Robert Spector offers a chilling look at today's retail environment. "Today, more than ever before, if a retailer is slow, it will be devoured by the swift; if it is ineffective, it will be outmaneuvered by the efficient." And then later in the same book: "Scores of mom-and-pop stores close their doors every day because they are unable — or not creative enough — to compete with national chains that employ advanced techniques ... ." (2)

My hope is that you use the Discovery Process as the advanced techniques to help your store thrive! For any individual retailer, thriving will be a matter of discovering where your opportunities lie, and discovering these opportunities will dictate that you become intimately familiar with your customers and their desires. Position yourself to meet those desires, and you're halfway home. Add to that strategy an attractive shopping environment that stimulates the senses, and you're three-quarters of the way there. Sprinkle in customer service that exceeds all expectations (*meeting* customer service expectations is taken for granted ... everybody does it), and you're getting even closer. Solve the riddle of how your store fits into its competitive arena, reexamine your advertising and pricing strategies based upon what you have learned, and voila! You can indeed increase the level of the success of your store. It won't be magic, but with a lot of hard work, improved profits is an obtainable goal.

Discovery alone is not enough. Once weaknesses are located, you must take action to correct or minimize the particular problems that are uncovered. You must act upon the opportunities the Discovery Process provides!

To say that the Discovery process will be easy would be a complete misstatement of fact, but if you are getting the jitters about the process, let me put your mind at rest with these two considerations. First, you need not undertake all of the exercises to benefit from just one of them. Even discovering one new element of the complex puzzle that is your store will be beneficial and, therefore, a good use of your time.

If, however, you're ready to tackle the full Discovery process, then you should think in terms of this metaphor: eating an elephant. No one, regardless of their size or the veracity of their appetite, is capable of eating an elephant in one, two, or even three sittings. Moreover, the elephant can only be eaten one bite at a time. If you tackle several of the elements of the Discovery Process, you should still do so one step at a time. And just as that elephant eater's appetite would most assuredly be satisfied after each meal, you will feel a certain satisfaction — you will simply become a better and smarter manager — with every nugget of new information that you gather and digest

In his book *From Good to Great,* Jim Collins wrote about what he and his team named "The Flywheel Theory." Collins and his research team tried to pin down the one thing that executives thought made their organizations reach what Collins characterized as the "tipping point," the point at which their organizations became great. (3)

After hours of interviews, however, Jim Collins' team concluded that there was never one thing or one vital decision, but rather, many small decisions, some that even seemed insignificant at the time, which ultimately made the *big* differences. They also concluded that these decisions were simply the byproduct of a clear overall vision of where the company was headed.

Collins likened their decision making processes to a huge flywheel, the shaft and wheel of a gigantic mechanism that is heavy and not easily moved. Each small positive decision and action caused the large wheel to rotate, but perhaps only a fraction of an inch. And, because those turning that heavy wheel were battling inertia, the first pushes were very hard. Eventually, with enough small pushes in the desired direction, the wheel began to speed up. At that point, the energy required to move the wheel was no greater than that which originally started the movement. The energy seemed to have more effect, however because of the increasing speed of the wheel. Eventually, as the flywheel continued to increase in speed, it supplied much of its own momentum.

Perhaps the Discovery Process will serve as a way to start your "flywheel" turning faster. It may be, as Collins's research suggests, that a series of small decisions will make all the difference.

Through the Discovery Process you will uncover information so that you can improve many facets of your business and don't overlook the small stuff. Do as Ed advised me so many years ago: Make sure that the *little* things do not go undone. Remember the lesson he taught and metaphorically speaking, pick up the nails that are scattered over your floor and put them back into the bin.

Chapter 1: Points to Remember

1. Remember the words of Wayne Dyer: "When you change the way you look at things, the things that you look at change." This mantra is especially true when you start examining your store from new perspectives.
2. The Discovery Process involves examining attributes of your operation in brand new ways.
3. The elements of the Discovery Process are most effective when used as a group, but you can benefit from using single elements.
4. Remember the metaphor of eating an elephant and undertake the Discovery Process "one bite at a time."
5. In Jim Collins book *From Good to Great*, the author asserts that it was the sum of many small points that made the "great companies" great. The managers of these companies said that some of the decisions even seemed insignificant at the time that they were made, but these decisions were always consistent with an overall goal.

CHAPTER 2

DISCOVERING: YOUR CUSTOMERS

The title of this chapter is somewhat ambiguous. On the one hand, discovering your customer suggests finding those customers that you are not currently serving. That, of course, is partially what the discussion in this chapter will be about, but it will also involve discovering what makes your current customers tick, or better yet, what motivates your customers to buy. In this sense, discovering your customer is more about discovering your customers' attributes. Who is your customer?

If you don't know the answer to this important question right now, don't feel like the Lone Ranger. But, without this knowledge you've probably been doing what you've wanted to do, buying the things that you wanted to sell with the belief that customers will simply show up and purchase those products from you. This so-called strategy is somewhat akin to the movie *Field of Dreams*, in which Kevin Costner's character was instructed to "build it and they will come." In the case of your business however, you would be better served to start thinking in terms of a strategy of: "Build what your customers want and they will come in larger numbers and spend more money." In order to do that, however you have to know who your customers are.

Here are a couple of examples of why this knowledge is important. We recently consulted with a home center retailer who said that 70 percent of his customers were contractors. That's important information, but the manager was quick to point out that he needs the other 30 percent and would even like to increase that number to help raise his operating margin.

And so we asked him the next logical question: "Of the remaining 30 percent, how many are male and how many are female?"

This brought a puzzled look as he responded, "Why is that important?"

We answered quickly: "There are several reasons."

It is a fact that single women are the second largest buying group (trailing only married couples) and the fastest growing segment of homeowners. If, by virtue of your store's environment or attributes, women feel uncomfortable shopping, you have narrowed your chances for finding success. You have turned your back on opportunity. Even when accompanied by their husbands, women are making nearly half of the choices when it comes to remodeling projects. In short, this is one demographic that no store operator dare ignore.

"OK," the storeowner said, "but just knowing women are *not* shopping in my store is not enough. How do I change that?" His question was right on and as you read through this book you'll learn the answer.

Another thing you should know about your customer base is: What is the average age of your shoppers? Consider this: The "Citibank Home Improvement Industry Report" says that Baby Boomers, who comprise the majority of the plus-55 demographic in the United States, account for more than half of all home-improvement expenditures today. That is a big number!

However, this segment of the population is growing older, and in areas where these demographic indicators align, installed sales are increasing at a commensurately rapid rate. In these areas, the old "Do It Yourself" (DIY) mentality is being replaced by the "Do It For Me" (DIFM) way of thinking. In fact, the Citibank report estimated that the DIFM market will be the fastest growing category in the home-improvement industry over the next 5 to 10 years. Does your customer base reflect this profile, and are you preparing for this increasing need for installed sales? Moreover, does your advertisement and store presentation convey a senior-friendly message?

OK let's set aside your current customer base for the moment and examine instead who your "ideal customer" would be. In this case we're not talking about physical attributes, of course, but rather a characterization of your ideal customer's age and sex in addition to their status as a homeowner, their income, educational levels, etc.

When you begin to profile your ideal customer, answer questions like the following: Does he work in town or does he commute? How far is his residence from my store? Is he likely to being moving to a different house in the near future or is he staying put?

The answers to questions like these are important for many reasons. I like to use the metaphor of trapping an animal. If, for instance, I want to trap a mouse, I know that a small piece of cheese is ideal bait and that, eventually, using that bait and patience, I will get the little gray varmint.

That same small piece of cheese, however, would have little success attracting a wild horse. The wild horse would simply not be interested in my small piece of cheese. It wouldn't motivate the horse. Cheese would be the wrong bait to attract a horse!

Now, I don't know that much about horses, but I would guess that, if I had one that trusted me, he might very well eat a small piece of cheese from my hand based upon his relationship with me. But if I wanted to bring him galloping across a pasture, I would use something else to attract him, a bucket of oats perhaps. That bait would be appropriate.

Simply put, before I set out to trap an animal, I need to know what animal I want to trap and then I need only know what bait will appeal to that kind of animal. Of course, this isn't rocket science, but in my experience, very few storeowners go through the process of identifying the ideal customer they want to "trap."

I'm not saying your customers are animals (although some of you might beg to differ!). I'm saying only that, in order to attract the customers that you want, you must know exactly who those customers are because that knowledge will affect what product you buy, how you merchandise that product, how you advertise that product, the ideal environment in which to showcase that product — the list goes on and on.

The process of profiling your ideal customer need not take days and days of endless thought and research. Quite the contrary, it can be a short and simple exercise.

One great way to start the process is to form a mental image of your top four or five customers and look for similar attributes in those people. Set aside your business accounts for the time being and look only at individuals. Now write down the common links between those people. If these are the people who are pleasant and profitable to deal with, it makes sense to try to generate more of them, doesn't it? It makes sense to try to *trap* this profile.

Once you have your ideal customer profile, use that information to brainstorm what would generally appeal to that group of people. Consider the charts that follow.

In the first example, a manager identified his store's ideal customer as male homeowners between the ages of 30 and 50 and living within 5 miles of the store. He then came up with the following observations about what would appeal to that group and what wouldn't:

Products	Environment	Background	Likes	Dislikes
Techno-Gadget	Bright, Happening	Music of the 70's-70's	NASCAR, hunting, fishing, competitive sports	Having to ask for help
Tools, New things	Smell of popcorn	Lots of visual stimulation	Promotions featuring sports	Spending time waiting to check out
Available rental for weekend projects	Product laid out in logical fashion	Something to eat	Relaxed informal invironment	Too much fanciness or "foo foo"

You can see that, by identifying his ideal customer, this manager even considered what music he should be playing in the store as part of setting bait to trap the right animal. Of course, other customers came into his store as well, but this manager is actively trying to attract his *ideal* customer through management by definitive action.

In the next example, a store manager determined that she wanted to attract couples. Because of her store's location close to a rather large retirement community, however, she placed the age that she wanted her business to appeal to at 45-65. Her ideal customers are homeowners as well, but they are probably more affluent than the customers of the store in the previous example.

Products	Environment	Background	Likes	Dislikes
Concentrate on upscale add-ons DIFM	Extremely clean	*Soft* easy listening music	Courteous customer service	Rude or unkempt clerks
Items creating convenience	Must be well-lighted	Accent lighting that sells by suggestion	Golf, gardening, leisure	Extreme colors for interior décor
Well-known quality brands	Easy access to clean restrooms	Subtle earth-tone decor	Being recognized	Being ignored

This simple exercise should give you hints about how to use the information you acquire from profiling your ideal customer. Make all of your decisions, thereafter, based upon that ideal customer group.

Kenneth Stone, Extension Economist and Professor of Economics at Iowa State University, said it this way: "Without a clear image of its target market, a small company tries to reach almost everyone and ends up appealing to almost no one!"

A short time ago, I overheard a conversation between a storeowner with whom I was working and one of his clerks. The clerk said that she missed the upbeat music that they used to play in the store. She even told the manager that some customers were saying they missed it as well. The manager explained that he had a couple of older customers complain about both the volume and the selection.

After overhearing this conversation, I pulled the manager aside and asked him if the ones who were complaining represented his ideal customer. He was quick to answer that, no, indeed, they did not!

After he completed the exercise and profiled his ideal customer, he immediately switched back to the music that appealed to a younger age group. This manager made a solid decision based upon the profiling he had done. He was managing by action and not reacting to isolated opinions.

It should be duly noted that there is the possibility that this manager alienated the older customers in this particular case, but as manager or owner of your business, you must determine what group your store should appeal to most. Remember what Mr. Stone said: Your store *will not* appeal to everybody — no store does.

Now that you have profiled your ideal customer and you have taken time to assess what he or she would prefer, look around your store and evaluate your present operation as regards how it dovetails (or doesn't) with the tastes and desires of your targeted ideal customer.

If you inherited your business, a previous operator or owner may have built your customer trap. If that is the case, you are probably still carrying and selling basically the same product mix that your predecessor offered. It is time for you to ask this very important question: Knowing the profile of my ideal customer, does my product offering fit the desires of my new profile group?

I worked with many stores during my years as a wholesaler of hardware products. I never once asked any of those operators to identify their ideal customer. Our company had a basic methodology for selecting the merchandise that would be in a store. The information was well founded and based upon some solid sales information, and truthfully, I think this wholesaler did, and still does, as good a job as any of their competitors in this regard. However, all of the stores we served ended up pretty much like all of the others, very cookie-cutter in regard to product assortment.

Sure, individual floor designs differed and environments varied, but product assortments didn't vary that much from location to location. Is it any wonder then that it was hard for those stores to differentiate themselves? If all of those stores were in exactly the same type of community with exactly the same quality of competition, catering to the same demographic parameters, and targeting exactly the same profile of customer, the cookie-cutter approach would have been right on. But such was not the case. It was simply a matter of the status quo and business as usual.

Ultimately, the owner or manager must make the decisions about product assortment and display. You have to shoulder the responsibility for determining what works best in your store, or in other words, you have to decide what bait best traps your animal.

Recently, our company was working with a client who saw the merit of customer profiling, but voiced this concern: his store was operating in a small town and he felt that he would have to attract shoppers of all profiles merely to survive. We cannot dispute the limitations of certain demographic realities, but the fact remains that structuring one's store to appeal to an ideal customer profile is beneficial nevertheless. It helps you, as a storeowner, maintain focus.

OK, now let's move from your ideal customer back to you current customers. It's time to discover who your current customers are. In order to do this, you must both observe them and ask them questions. The questions will vary from situation to situation, but there are some that should always be included. For instance, doesn't it seem like an elemental question to ask your customer what they think of your store? It does to me. It's not a unilateral relationship, you know. No transaction is one-sided. Yes, you are selling products to the public, but more importantly (hopefully), your customer is buying those products. It is worth remembering that the customer has the biggest dog in this fight for they control where their money is spent.

Asking questions does little good, however unless you ask a sizeable number of people. It is simply a matter of having enough information from which to draw informative conclusions.

But there are a couple of issues that complicate the process. First and perhaps foremost, the chances are good that you are not going to get completely truthful answers. Many of your regular customers will not tell you and/or your employees what they really think. They either value the relationship too highly or simply do not have the intestinal fortitude to be truthful when asked their opinion of your operation. However, if an outsider asks the same questions and assures the respondent of anonymity, he is far more likely to receive the kinds of answers you need — unbiased answers that will provide you with the greatest insight.

Therefore, it is important that you outline the process with some independent group, our company perhaps, or maybe a college class or fraternity/sorority. At any rate, let me repeat: Do not attempt the Discovery Process customer surveys by yourself or with regular employees! It will not work! Not only because of the truthfulness factor but also because you must maintain customer service regardless of whatever else you have going on in your store. Surveys require a substantial time commitment, and your employees should stay at their everyday tasks.

Although it is clear that you should use an outside source for conducting the interviews, it will be up to you to design them. The questions must be as succinct as possible and yet comprehensive enough to provide the answers that you want to learn.

One very important factor to be aware of while you are planning your interview process is your customers' time. In this day and age, when many demands are placed on everybody's time, respecting this priceless element is important indeed. Therefore, interviews must be short.

In our discussion of the interview process, let's split the interviews into three categories: entrance, exit, and random telephone.

With entrance interviews we suggest that observation be used to learn as much about your customers as possible. Therefore, the survey sheet examples below include both methodologies, interview and observation. In example A-1, for instance, only the bottom three questions require answers from the interviewees. These sections are in bold type and underlined.

We have found questions regarding age to be delicate for some interviewees, and consequently, in our survey, age groups are blocked into decades, which ameliorates the avoidance effect for the interviewer. Still, the safest way to approach this information is a "best guess" strategy. After all, you are only trying to learn the average age of your customer base in order that you might compare that against your ideal customer profile.

The interview process itself might go something like this: *Hi folks. Welcome to Fletcher Hardware. May I ask you four or five questions today? How far is your home from the store? What is your zip code? Are you shopping for something specific? Did you try our store 1st, 2nd or 3rd to find this item? Are you a professional or homeowner? Thanks. I hope we can ask you a couple of questions after you shop. Please return this number when you leave the store and I will have a small gift for your participation in our survey today.*

The simple form on the following page is an example of one that could be easily completed.

Entrance Survey Form A-1

Time Information: ____:____ a.m. ☐ p.m. ☐

Day: Monday ☐ Tuesday ☐ Wednesday ☐
Thursday ☐ Friday ☐ Saturday ☐ Sunday ☐

Date: _____

Shopper Gender:

Male ☐ Female Couple ☐ Two Men ☐ Two Women ☐

Approximate Age of Shoppers:

20-30 ☐ ☐ 30-40 ☐ ☐ 40-50 ☐ ☐
50-60 ☐ ☐ 60+ ☐ ☐

Shoppers Residence:

Less than 1 mile ☐ ☐ 1 to 5 miles ☐ ☐
5 to 10 miles ☐ ☐ 10 to 15 miles ☐ ☐
15 to 20 miles ☐ ☐ 20+ miles ☐ ☐

Zip Code _____

General Information:

Shopping for something specific? Yes ☐ No ☐
If yes, shopped this store? 1st ☐ 2nd ☐ 3rd ☐

Shopper Type:

Professional ☐ Homeowner ☐

Shopper Tracking Number: _____

You will notice that the question regarding the shopper's gender treats a couple as a "group." Of course, a form could be filled out for each shopper in that group, but we have found it difficult to separate the data in the instance of husband and wife interviewees.

With the information gleaned from this short interview and the observations that have been made by the interviewer, we have a nice entry for our customer profile even though we took only a small amount of the customer's time.

Notice that both the entrance and exit survey forms have a line to enter a tracking number. This is done solely for the purpose of timing the shopper's in-store experience. We have found that this can be done with theater-type tickets or handwritten numbers. The important thing is to assure that the entrance and exit times are assigned to the same individual.

Later, in a chapter dealing with environment, we will outline the process for observing the customer's movement and activities while he or she is inside the store. But for now, let us assume that our shopper has concluded his shopping experience and is ready to exit the building. In the following example (A-2), you will see a simple yet revealing exit survey.

Notice that we are not trying to learn everything about every customer. That would, of course, be impossible. What we are trying to do is develop a profile of who is currently shopping in your store, when they shop, how long it takes, and the opinion of the shopper regarding the visit.

Exit Survey Form A-2

Time Information: ____:____   a.m. ☐   p.m. ☐

Shopping Experience:

Did you find what you were looking for?   Yes ☐   No ☐

If yes, did you buy it?   Yes ☐   No ☐

If no, was it a pricing issue?   Yes ☐   No ☐

If you didn't find the item, what were you looking for? _____

_____

Would you rate your shopping experience as?

Unpleasant ☐   OK ☐   Pleasant ☐   Extremely Pleasant ☐

Shopper Tracking Number: _____

    The exit survey, like the entrance survey is short and to the point. It takes very little of the customer's time and yet provides you with a wealth of information.

    On election night, I am always amazed at how quickly the statisticians predict the outcome of the contest. Based on very small samples derived from exit polls, they draw conclusions, predict winners and losers, and do so with a reasonable amount of accuracy. Our process is similar. You only need to collect data from your shoppers for a few days to have a reasonable representation of your current customer base profile. As with any statistical study, however, the larger the test sample the more accurate the results will be.

    After you conclude the exit survey, it is a good idea to offer the survey participants a small token of appreciation for the time they have traded. If your store's name happens to be on the gift, a koozie perhaps, or cap or small tool, anything that has perceived value, then so much the better.

I promised that I would discuss random telephone interviews. I enjoy this type of interaction with a store's customers and I have found it to be perhaps the most enlightening of the interview processes that I have discussed. Phone interviews, because of the anonymity involved seem to produce even more poignant answers, than do the face-to-face encounters of the entrance and exit surveys. Another thing that I have noticed when making these calls is that the customer views the interaction as flattering. Not all, of course, but many respondents comment that they are surprised that the store being studied is that interested in their opinion. I feel that something beneficial is generated from that reaction alone. Perhaps it signals to those customers that the store is really trying to meet their needs.

During the phone interviews, we often use questions regarding customer service, the store's environment, and pricing perceptions to generate an even clearer picture of who the store's customer is and what they would like to see from the store. Remember that time is still the critical consideration, but I have found that many customers, once asked, like to share their opinions.

One final thought regarding phone surveys, when compiling your call lists, pick both current customers and customers that no longer shop your store if you have that information. It can be enlightening to hear what has changed a former customer's shopping habits.

OK, we've gathered the information, now let's examine why this information is so critical. At the beginning of this chapter, I wrote that we would discuss the process of attracting new customers. Here's a newsflash. Attracting new customers is not so easy to do. Malcolm Gladwell, the renowned author of *The Tipping Point* and *Blink*, put it thusly: "As the retail market grows more cutthroat, storeowners have come to realize that it's all but impossible to increase the number of customers coming in, and have concentrated instead on getting the customers they do have to buy more." (4)

If we assume that the first part of Mr. Gladwell's statement is true (I am convinced that it is), then the last part of his statement becomes paramount in importance: *You must concentrate on getting the customers you do have to buy more.*

A proven way to get customers to buy more is to increase their shop time and, by making your store more appealing to your ideal customer, you will do just that. That point should bring this whole chapter full circle and clarify the urgent need to identify both your ideal and your current customer profile.

Chapter 2: Points to Remember

1. Your current customer base is not necessarily your "ideal" customer base.
2. To attract your ideal customer, you must know what "bait" to use. Before you can know what bait to use, you must recognize who your ideal customer is.
3. Once you know who your ideal customer is, that knowledge can guide you through tailoring the proper assortment, advertising, and promotion ideas for that customer and even the environmental attributes of your store that will best showcase the products.
4. Your store will not appeal to every consumer.
5. A great way to know what customers think is to ask them. The most effective way to get honest opinions is to have unbiased surveyors asking the questions.
6. It is easier to develop additional business with existing customers than it is to gain new customers.

Chapter 2: Action Steps

1. Gather your key personnel and compile a composite that characterizes your "ideal" customer.
2. After you have developed this ideal customer image, discuss the way that your store currently appeals to this ideal customer. Discuss the attributes of your store that will not appeal to this segment. Have your personnel suggest ways in which you might further "bait the trap" for your ideal customer.
3. Determine how well your ideal customer base dovetails with your current customer base and discuss transitional ideas to get your store to where it needs to be.
4. Contact an outside agency and plan interview processes. The interviews should be completed as customers enter and exit your store. In addition, schedule random telephone surveys. Compile your information.

Chapter 3

DISCOVERING: POTENTIAL IN EXISTING CUSTOMERS

As we discussed in the previous chapter, there are many experts who believe that increasing the number of new customers coming through your store's door is becoming progressively more difficult. Advertising budgets are stretched in an attempt to accomplish this daunting task. During periods of intense advertising, store traffic should, and often does, increase, but determining how much of the increase is due to new customers, and the even more difficult task of turning those people into repeat customers, is an entirely different topic for discussion.

Why is it so hard to attract new people into your store? There is no one simple answer, of course — that would be too easy. Rather, your store's dynamics and environment, the trade area within which it operates, and its competition are all part of this equation. However, one of the changes that has had the biggest impact on the retail industry as a whole is simply the growth of consumer choice.

Consider this: Malcolm Gladwell wrote that, "The amount of selling space per American shopper is now more than double what it was in the mid-seventies, meaning that profit margins have never been narrower, and costs of starting a business — and of failing — have never been higher." (1)

The sales space number that he referenced was a staggering statistic back then and now, more than ten years later, the trend that he observed has only accelerated. Shopping centers and additional freestanding retail stores are popping up, in and around metropolitan areas. This trend of increasing retail sales space, and the lure for your customers, is very likely to continue.

As if these changing dynamics weren't enough, the competitive nature of retail pricing that Gladwell observed continues its increasingly voracious digestion of profit opportunities. Part of this scenario, no doubt, is attributable to the increase of physical retail space that we just discussed. Add the availability of easy price comparisons and Internet shopping, and it is easy to understand the continued erosion of margins and profits.

Although rural-area retailers might, at first glance, seem isolated from these elements, I assure you that such is not the case. The Internet, after all, is available everywhere. In addition, as our company works with these rural storeowners we listen to them lament their customers' daytrips to big-box outlets, where selections are larger and pricing is perceived to be lower. It is apparent that the increased ease of communication and mobility have yielded this incredible "shrinking world" phenomenon for retailers.

Given these parameters, it makes sense to focus on your *current* customer base and thereby maximize your return from your *existing* opportunities. We have already discussed making your store more appealing to your ideal customer, and that strategy is the springboard for this philosophy.

Now let's analyze the opportunities for increasing profits from your *existing* customer base by isolating key points.

1. **Increasing the frequency of same customer visits**
   Simply increasing the number of times your current customers shop in your store will increase their purchases. We will discuss this in Chapter 11 during our examination of advertising.

2. **Increasing shop time during those visits**
   This number directly correlates with the shopping experience and will be discussed further in this chapter and also in the chapters on customer service and environment.

3. **Increasing margin dollars per ticket**
   Margin percentage and total ticket size affect this factor, which will be discussed in the chapters on customer service, competition, and profitability.

4. **Increasing line count per ticket**

I will discuss this factor in the customer service and environmental modules as it is primarily affected by selection, a proactive approach to suggestive selling, and the length of time a shopper spends in your store.

5. **Increasing conversion rates**

Increasing your conversion rate holds one of the greatest opportunities for retailers of all descriptions as it is a measurable and improvable matrix. Conversion rate will be the topic of discussion for the balance of this chapter.

Most retailers measure and track their transaction or ticket counts. This is valuable information, but during our consultative conversations with those retailers they often refer to this number as their traffic count. When their transactions are down, they say simply that their traffic is down. They may be right or they may be wrong. For you see, merely knowing the number of tickets or transactions completed over a given time period tells only part of the story.

A greater indicator of the day's, week's, or month's success is the conversion rate. The conversion rate is simply the ratio of the number of sales tickets divided by the number of people who walked into your store or, said another way, conversion rate is results divided by opportunities.

Let's take a look at how this works.

Time Period	Traffic Count	Transactions	Conversion Factor	Conversion Percentage
A	125	75	.60	60%
B	118	82	.69	69%

You can see that, if the merchant was tracking his transaction count in the example above and calling that number his traffic count, he would mistakenly report that his traffic had increased from time period A to time period B. The truth is, this transaction count was up—transactions went from 75 to 82 — but his traffic count was down as it went from 125 to 118. This difference is the key point of conversion rate.

During the time period A, only 60 percent of the people who walked into his store actually bought something. For the period of measurement referenced in period B, that number increased to 69 percent.

To figure conversion rate, you must have a denominator, the number of people (opportunities) that walk into your store. Having access to this number obviously requires traffic counters, which are electronic devices that perform the customer counting function. These counters can range from the very simple and relatively inexpensive to pricey. The latter are linked to computers with software that analyzes reported data in various ways. The better units will have directional counting capability, which is convenient, of course, but the simpler units still provide the valuable denominator that we are looking for.

Let's say, for the sake of discussion, that you have installed traffic counters and have identified your denominator. How then do you work toward increasing your conversion rate?

Don't mistake conversion rate for a lack of suggestive selling. In the traditional sense, suggestive selling implies add-on sales and is associated with increased dollars per transaction. For example, let's say that a clerk asked a customer who was about to buy a can of paint if she had all of the brushes she needed. Perhaps the clerk also suggested some new type of masking tape. If by this effort the clerk increased the sale, the dollars-per-transaction measurement increased but not the conversion rate.

In the example above, the customer buys the *extra* brush or tape that the clerk was pushing. The customer was already going to buy *something* however, and therefore the conversion rate was unaffected. Yes, the dollars per transaction were increased, and obviously that is a very good thing, *but only selling something to those prospects who otherwise would have purchased nothing increases conversion rate.*

Therefore, the greatest opportunity lies in simultaneously increasing dollars per transaction and conversion rate. Let's discuss, for a moment, the hypothetical situation represented in the chart below. I have chosen simple numbers for easy computation.

Outcome	Traffic Count	Ticket Count	Conversion Rate	$ Per Ticket	Sales
A	100	75	75%	10.00	750.00
B	100	80	80%	10.00	800.00
C	100	80	80%	9.00	720.00

Let's say that each of the three rows above represents different possible outcomes for the same period of time. The customer count, therefore, will remain constant at 100 people.

In example A, 75 tickets were written. Therefore, the conversion rate is 75 percent, or the ticket count of 75 divided by the traffic count of 100. The average dollar amount per transaction was $10.00, which is achieved by dividing the period's sales of $750 by the ticket count of 75.

In example B, you will notice a different scenario. The potential was the same because the customer count remained constant. In this example, we wrote 80 tickets and our conversion rate was 80 percent, or 80 tickets divided by 100 customers. Our average ticket size was the same, or $10 per transaction. Therefore, the same 100 prospects that walked through the door generated $50 more in sales simply by virtue of the fact that we increased our conversion rate.

But now let's look at the last row of the chart, outcome C, and consider this possibility. In this example, our conversion rate remains at 80 percent. When we contrast just the first and last lines of the chart, we notice a higher conversion rate of 80 percent compared to 75 percent. But notice that our average dollars per transaction decreased, going from $10 to $9. Therefore, our sales over the period were lower than in the first example, even though our conversion rate was higher.

I have heard it espoused in discussions with clients that, if they simply try to sell *something* to a person who would have otherwise bought nothing, there is a likelihood that the dollars per transaction will decrease. I see their point given the formula, but if you sell *anything* to somebody who would have otherwise purchased nothing, it is a good thing regardless of mathematical averages. A five-dollar item sold means five dollars that you will deposit. *Don't let any benchmarks take your focus away from the fact that ultimately you deposit dollars and dollars only, not conversion rates, not dollars per transaction, or any other mathematical measurement.*

Your conversion rate, as with your dollars per transaction, is simply a clue to help you track the effectiveness of your efforts. I would suggest, however, that an increased conversion rate would always yield the ultimate prize of increased deposited dollars. So how do we accomplish this feat?

Once again, the answer is that there are many answers. First of all let's look at what must happen in order for a sale (or from the customer's perspective, a purchase) to occur.

The shopper comes into your store either for (A.) something specific or (B.) simply to browse (perhaps to kill time or to see what is new and available). Let's begin with those in group A. The shopper has this preconceived set of perceptions:

1. He knows what he wants.
2. He knows where he thinks he should be able to find that item or items.
3. He is time-conscious of both his need and of the product's availability.
4. He has an acceptable price range for the item in question.

The equation for a sale to take place might then be stated thusly from a retailer's perspective:

If (D=S), If (PS=L2), If (TN=TA) and If (APR=P) then the customer will make a purchase and (more importantly) you will make a sale.

Broken down by elements, it goes like this. The customer's Desire must equal your Selection. His Position in Space must equal both your geographical Location and the Location within your store at which the product is displayed. The Timeliness of his Need must equal the Timeliness of the Availability of your product. And finally the customer's Acceptable Price Range must equal your Price.

Does this way of thinking complicate the issue? Quite the contrary, understanding all of the elements in the equation allows you to increase the likelihood of improving your store's performance. The equation itself, of course, is simply a vehicle to deliver the understanding. It is absolutely *not* important to quote the equation or remember it verbatim, but instead, you should simply focus on the inherent message in this equation and grasp its elements, which are discussed in isolation below.

The first part of the equation — if Desire equals Selection — means that, if a customer comes in looking for something specific and you don't have what he is looking for, and he is unwilling to wait for you to order the item, then there's no way he's going to buy that item from you. A sale can't happen.

Therefore, it is obviously important to know who's coming into your store and what they are expecting, and hence, the importance of surveys. This ties in quite nicely with profiling your ideal customer as well. Remember? Your product selection should reflect your ideal customer's desires. Consequently, your selection will match your customers' specific wants or needs more frequently. The cycle then comes full circle, and your conversion rate increases.

The second element — the customer's Position in Space must align with both the Location of your store and the Location of the desired merchandise within your store — tells us that location actually consists of two elements. The location of your store is a topic for another discussion. At this point, let us focus instead on the location of the merchandise within your store. If you have the item in stock, will your customer find it?

Wait a minute, you might say. If we have what he wants, we're going to tell him where it is. You will, that is, if you get a chance to wait on him. You will, that is, if he doesn't come in at the same time as six other people and when there are only three clerks working the floor. You will, that is, if she's not the quiet type, who says, when approached, "No thanks. I'm just looking."

So the location of merchandise in your store is of paramount importance, and this location is actually more than simply the gondola on which it resides, although that is one consideration regarding this element, of course.

The location of an item is actually a three dimensional field. Yes, that's right. Your merchandise location consists of three dimensions. An item must be displayed within the department in which it is expected to be displayed, which is old news, of course, but important nonetheless. And here the plot thickens, because your customer's expectation of the logical location is a subjective assessment. Is there more than one place that a person might expect to find a particular item or items? Of course there is, and that is the very purpose for an old concept known as cross-merchandising. You will likely increase your conversion rate if you display items in each of the areas a customer might expect them to be found

Let me give you an example of how all of this affected a shopping experience for me recently. I have been building a home theater. On a recent trip to my daughter's home, she showed me the luminous stars that she had placed on the ceiling of my granddaughter's bedroom. I liked them! I thought that they would be interesting on the black ceiling of the room housing my home theater, and so I set out to find them, looking in hobby stores, decorating centers, and eventually Wal-Mart. No luck. No stars.

In the hobby and craft section of the local Wal-Mart, I looked and looked until I finally became convinced that they simply did not have any luminous stars. No clerk was available that night (surprise, surprise), and so my desire for stars went unrealized. Eventually, my longing for stars subsided and I became quite content to live without stars on my theater ceiling.

So now let's fast-forward a few weeks. I went into Wal-Mart again, but this time to buy a toy for my grandson for his birthday. Lo and behold, what did I discover in the toy department? You guessed it! Stars, packages and packages of luminous stars! I could have literally reconstructed the Milky Way with the stars at Sam's place. But I didn't buy them.

The buying equation broke down in two specific places. The first failure occurred in the location portion of the equation. I was in the Wal-Mart store, but the stars were not displayed in the location that seemed most logical to me. Therefore, my Position in Space equaled the Location of the store, but it did not equal the Location of the luminous stars within the store. I did not, nor do I currently, consider the stars to be toys, although that is the department where I ultimately found them.

The other breakdown occurred in the Timeliness of Need must equal Timeliness of Availability part of the equation. I had a need for the stars the night I was looking for them (of course, in this case, need is loosely defined and D for Desire could easily be substituted), but they were not available. They were in the store, of course, but I didn't find them — until later, but by then I had talked myself out of using them. When I had the need, they were not available. When they *were* available, I no longer had the need. The elements of the equation were not fulfilled.

I don't remember if I bought anything else the night that I was looking for the stars but could not find them. I doubt it, for I was on a quest to find the stars. If I *didn't* buy anything else, though, Wal-Mart's conversion rate was lower that day than it could have been if the elements of the equation had been fulfilled. If I *did* buy something else, their per-ticket transaction dollar amount was lower than it could have been. Either way, it's a few bucks of mine that they didn't deposit. Either way, they lose.

OK, remember that was just *my* experience. Multiply that times the other people who, similarly, did not find the product that they wanted because it was not where they expected it to be, and you can begin to appreciate the size of the unrealized opportunities.

As an aside, I have noticed that in many stores of this type the checkout personnel will now sometimes ask, "Did you find everything that you were looking for?" I can tell you without qualification or reservation, however, that I did not and I would not ask about the stars at the checkout and reinitiate the futile odyssey.

Remember, I said that the placement of merchandise was actually a three dimensional point in space. I expected to find the stars in the craft department. At the moment, I don't know why. That's just the location that made sense to me, and so the point at which those stars were located in the store was far different from what I expected. But let's say for the sake of discussion that I had found the right aisle and I was standing in front of the gondola that displayed the stars.

There is still one axis, the vertical, which we have not discussed. It just so happens that, when I did find the correct point along the length of the correct gondola, my eyes fell easily upon the luminescent stars. They were displayed at about eye level in a zone that we call the *Reflex Zone*, the area on the vertical axis from 30" above the floor to 60" above the floor. This eye-level zone is an area through which the eyes easily and quickly travel, and is the primary real estate along the side of any gondola.

Doesn't it make sense that the items that are purchased most frequently in any given department lay within this zone? It will certainly make it easier to find those items. The more shoppers who find these items, the more who will buy them. Therefore, by adhering to a rule of merchandising, placing your best-selling items within the reflex zone, you will increase your conversion rate.

I have heard others suggest that a merchant should place his slower moving items in the reflex zone and make the customer look and bend for the better selling items. Although I can see the rationale for this thought process, I believe that you stand to lose more than you gain if customers do not conveniently locate the items they are looking for.

In fact, some grocery stores are now experimenting with merchandising on three eye levels, placing items that appeal to children low on the gondolas while the mid-level merchandising is structured to appeal to women and the top to men. This process optimizes the ease with which each of these subgroups finds the items they desire.

At the beginning of this discussion, I mentioned that there are two types of shoppers that come into your store. I characterized them thusly: (A.) those looking for something specific and (B.) those killing time, browsing to see what's new. All of the discussion thus far has been on group A. Let's now consider those shoppers in group B.

One distinction comes immediately to the forefront. Those in group A are looking for something specific. Therefore, it is *hypothetically* possible to achieve a 100 percent conversion rate with this group. If you had what each of those people wanted, if they found it, and if they were satisfied with the price, the transaction would likely occur.

But we must view the second group in a completely different light. If a customer is simply killing time, then our best chance of selling him *anything* lies in selling him impulse items. If the person is browsing, it is likely that they are contemplating a purchase of a specific item or items in the future. They want to see how your selection or pricing dovetails with their expectations or desires.

In this particular example, the Timeliness of Need element is not yet in play. The very fact that they are browsing for this item or group of items indicates that the time of need is approaching, however. Perhaps their exposure to your pricing and selection will move them into Group A on their next visit.

In both the time-killer and the browser scenarios, the likelihood of selling them *anything* correlates with the amount of time they spend in your store. They are more likely to see something that they want to buy impulsively if they see more of the items that your store offers. The longer they are in the store, the more things they will see, and so we want all of our shoppers to linger longer.

It is true that shoppers tend to look for convenient easy-in, easy-out shopping. The convenience store industry is built around — indeed categorically named for — this one characteristic desire of all shoppers. However, if you can offer your customers that kind of convenience but through an inviting and interesting layout and environment, you also increase their shop time you have, indeed, won the retail lottery. Increased shop time, if it is generated because of a pleasant shopping experience (instead of poor customer service), almost always correlates with increased purchases. You have given your customers what they desire and simultaneously gotten what you wanted

We will discuss increasing shop time in detail in the section on store environment. For the moment, however, begin to think of a customer's trip into your store as a sensory-laden event. Would your customers say that your store, as John Denver poetically sang, "fills up my senses"?

Remember that your customer will register how your store looks, how it sounds, and how it smells. He can be influenced by things to taste and touch as well, and it is the sum of his sensory experience along with his interaction with your crew that will determine the way he "feels" about his visit to your store.

Your layout either communicates a welcoming feel or it doesn't. Your lighting will either draw attention to those things that you feel are most important in your store, as well as guide people through your store, or it won't. Your signage should declare your policies and your values. These environmental elements and many more will homogenize into your customers' *feeling* about your store.

People shop where they feel best, where they *feel* most comfortable, where they *feel* most intrigued or most engaged. They shop where they *feel* like they receive their best value and where they *feel* like they receive the best service. In regards to increasing shop time, it's obviously *all* about how your customers *feel*!

Chapter 3: Points to Remember

1. It is more difficult to develop new customers than it is to increase your business and profit from your existing customer base.
2. You can increase business and profit from existing customers by:
   a. Increasing the frequency of same customer visits
   b. Increasing the shop time of existing customers
   c. Increasing margin dollars per ticket
   d. Increasing the line count per ticket
   e. Increasing your store's conversion rate
3. The terms "ticket count" and "conversion rate" are not synonymous. To compute your store's conversion rate requires a denominator, which is the number of people who walked through the door on a given day. The number of tickets written divided by the number of opportunities (people who walked in) equals the conversion rate.
4. Suggestive selling does not necessarily increase conversion rate. Suggestive selling in the traditional sense refers to increasing ticket line counts. In order to increase your conversion rate, you must sell something to a patron who would have otherwise bought nothing.

There are many elements to the sales equation. A customer's desire must equal your selection, his point in space must equal both the physical location of your store plus the location of the merchandise within your store, and his time of need must equal the time of your product's availability. And finally, his acceptable price range must encompass your price.

Chapter 3: Action Steps

1. Call your key personnel together and review the above key points. Focus on key point number two and use it to begin a dialogue with your employees. Start formulating a strategy to address each of the sub-points. For example, regarding point 2a, discuss ways of attracting your regular customers back into your store more frequently. This might include ideas like giving out coupons that are good for purchases made over the next week only. Adding this sense of urgency to the offer will likely persuade some of them to come back into the store before they would have done so otherwise. Continue this process on each of the subsequent points, asking for input from your team.

2. Explore the possibility of procuring traffic counters for your doors and start planning the implementation of conversion rate measurement. When employees know that you are measuring this important matrix, they will strive to improve it!

DISCOVERING: LAYOUT WEAKNESSES

You communicate with your customers in a number of ways, including through advertisement, product selection and display. You also communicate through your employees and signage, and your support of the community — the list goes on and on.

Perhaps it's not quite as obvious as these other examples, but you also communicate with your customers through the environmental attributes of your store. For example, your lighting, which can convey a welcoming feeling and guide people to the products you want them to see. You communicate *your feelings* about your store through the level of maintenance and the degree of cleanliness and order that you uphold. You also communicate how you want people to walk through your store and, through its design, what you want them to focus on as they do. Consequently, there are no more important elements in communication with your customer than your store's environment and layout.

But wait a minute, you might say. People have been shopping here for years and it's always been good enough; they know where to find things, and besides, they don't like change. Gosh, if I make even a small change, some of them complain. They start saying, "You're just like Wal-Mart, always changing things."

Oh, if it were only true and, in regard to change, we *were* just like Wal-Mart!

Remember in the previous chapter we talked about keeping people in the store longer and how that would affect your store's conversion rate for the better? One way to communicate to your regular customers that you want them to stay in your store longer is precisely to change things.

If they are familiar with seeing the same products in the same places and displayed the same way, they will not linger long, I assure you. Take those same products, put them in different locations and highlight them in different ways, and suddenly you engage your customers' attention. As we talked about earlier, you fill up their senses. Simultaneously, their shop time increases, and the likelihood that they will find things that they didn't even know you had does as well. I can't tell you how many times dealers have told me about long-time customers marveling at the many new things in the store after a reset — even though no product was actually added during the process.

But wait a minute, the astute observer might say. I can't rearrange my store everyday, every week, or even every month. Of course not, and that's not what we're proposing, but rather, this is meant to encourage you to consider how long it's been since you have undertaken a major overhaul of your store's sales space. If it has been over four or five years, then it has been too long, and your store is wallowing in the self-imposed limitations of mediocrity. It's time for a change!

But change is expensive, you might cry. To which I will answer, "Yes, it is." But how expensive is it to grow stagnant? How expensive is it to watch your customers migrate to stores that are more exciting, more engaging, or more up to date?

And which expense, remodeling or stagnation, would more positively affect your attitude and the attitudes of those who work with you and for you? I have witnessed unbelievable metamorphoses of employees' attitudes in stores where the sales floor has been updated and the selling environment improved. A synergistic enthusiasm engulfs crews as they emerge on the other side of such an undertaking.

Which expense, remodeling or stagnation, would more positively affect your store's trend lines into the future? Yes, changing and updating your store is expensive, but your store is constantly evolving one way or the other. Your operation is either growing stronger or it's growing weaker. I encourage you, therefore, to take a pro-active approach to your store's evolution. Become the master of your store's fate, so to speak.

Are you thinking that this level of change is such a daunting task that you do not know where or how to begin? It's not an easy undertaking, I'll grant you that! However, remember the metaphor that I used earlier: eating an elephant. It can only be done one bite at a time. This project should be undertaken in the same spirit.

Let's steal a thought from the old *The Sound of Music* song "Do-Re-Mi." Maria sang, "Let's start at the very beginning. A very good place to start."

It's a cute song, and in the case of retrofitting your store, it's good advice. The beginning, in this case, probably lies in securing a floor-plan designer. Many wholesalers have departments that offer these services. Distributors often have groups of floor designs that they try to modify to fit all store shapes and sizes. *But for design services that position the wholesaler's interest secondary to your own, an outside designer is the better choice.*

Our company undertakes the design process in a unique and more scientific way than most. We spend time evaluating the current floor plan and assess what is working well and what isn't. We learn all that we can learn from studying traffic flow through the current layout, and then we analyze that information and digest input from the storeowner and manager. Only after this much research do we undertake the actual design process.

It is important that your store's design communicates your desired flow of traffic through the store. We endeavor to deepen the average penetration of customers into the store's various sections using an evaluation system that divides the store into 12 zones. Remember, deeper penetration into the store typically equates with increased shop time, which in turn correlates with increased ticket size and conversion rate. It makes a lot of sense to develop a strategy to increase your PDQ®

Penetration and Dispersion Quotient ® (PDQ)

Penetration and Dispersion Quotient® (PDQ) is a benchmark for analyzing your success in maximizing the use of your available sales space. In an ideal world, 100 percent of your customers would shop through 100 percent of the departments or sectors of your store.

Although that is unlikely to happen, it is, in fact, at least *hypothetically* possible.

Whether or not this lofty goal is ever reached, it certainly makes sense to aspire to producing better traffic flow throughout the entirety of your store. Doesn't it make sense that customers who are exposed to more products will buy more? That is what we are after.

Penetration analysis is not new. Its study should probably be attributed to Paco Underhill, who has devoted his life to the study of why shoppers buy and how they react within the selling environment. His company, Envirosell, is recognized worldwide for quality research and scientific retail analysis.

Our system is dramatically different, however, from the systems that pre-date it. Our system divides a store's sales space into 12 sectors labeled simply A through L. After the study, the sectors are then ranked according to penetration.

There will often be *at least* one sector that receives 100 percent penetration, the sector in which the main entrance and exit doors reside. In order to enter your store, if it has only one entrance, every customer has to penetrate that sector. Beyond that observation, however, nothing is assured. There is a likelihood that the sector that houses the customer service area and the one to the right of the entrance door will receive the next highest levels of penetration, but that too varies according to retail situations and layouts.

After charting the flow of traffic through a store, (typically the charting procedure lasts at least a full day), the results are entered into a computer application to determine the PDQ. The structure of the equation is dynamic. The sectors are ranked according to penetration, with the least value assigned to those sectors that are penetrated most often, such as the entry point, cash wrap, and customer service desk. These sectors win by default and, therefore, the multiplier assigned to the penetration of those zones and used in the analysis is much lower.

Conversely, higher values are assigned to the sectors that are penetrated least often. Each time the analysis is done, the sectors are reassigned post-study values based upon their penetration during that period. Because of this dynamic element, the study will be relevant and equitable regardless of seasonality and changes in departmental layouts. This strategy also assures the researcher that a compiled benchmark from store to store is an informative comparison as to the efficient use of sales space of the contrasted stores.

Let's take a closer look at how our system works:

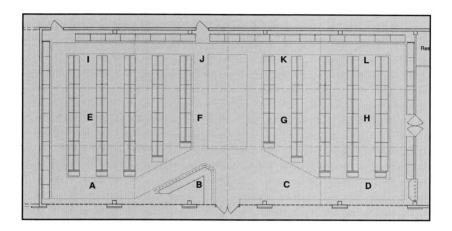

As you can see, we have divided this store drawing into 12 sectors, each labeled A through L. The order in which we assign the letters is unimportant as, after the study, they are reassigned a value based upon their penetration, but in this case, we simply labeled left to right, front to back. You will notice that the front doors reside in sectors B and C. The customer service area is housed in sector B as well.

After assigning each sector its letter label, we print copies of the drawing equal to one-quarter of the average traffic count. For example, if the average traffic count was 120, we would print 30 sheets. This will allow us to track the traveled path of four shoppers on each sheet. You could do more per sheet, but the easier the traffic paths are to follow on the pages, the easier it is to interpret and extract the data from the sheet and enter it in the spreadsheet.

The following inset is the same floor plan with the paths two shoppers followed illustrated with dashed lines. Notice that shopper one turned right upon entrance and contacted sectors C, G, K, D, H and B. The other shopper entered sectors C, G, K, J, F and B.

In this very small sampling then, our study would indicate 100 percent penetration in four sectors of the store: C, G, B and K.

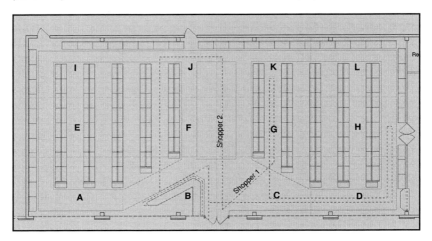

The following insert is a screenshot of the spreadsheet we use to determine the PDQ with the zone penetration information for the shoppers represented in the drawing above. These entries are logged with X's into the squares beneath the corresponding zone letters. The rest of the computations are done automatically.

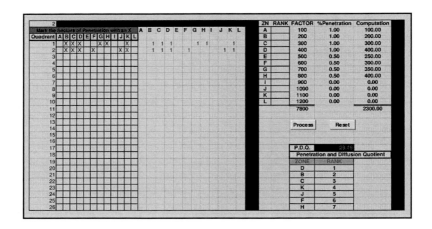

After we have entered all of the information into the spreadsheet and activated the Process button, the application sorts the zones by the number of customers who entered those zones and ranks them in descending order. You can see that zones G, C, B and K ranked as zones 1 through 4 in penetration. In this abbreviated example, both of the shoppers in our study entered into those zones and therefore there was 100 percent penetration of those areas.

The square in the upper left-hand corner of the spreadsheet displays the number 2, which is simply a count of the number of customers tracked through the store.

As I stated earlier, we assigned the zones with the highest penetration percentages the lowest values. Penetration into these zones requires less effort, and therefore, we assigned these zones the lower values. What follows are the multiplying factors assigned to each zone based upon its rank of penetration.

Zone 1	100	Zone 5	500	Zone 9	900
Zone 2	200	Zone 6	600	Zone 10	1000
Zone 3	300	Zone 7	700	Zone 11	1100
Zone 4	400	Zone 8	800	Zone 12	1200

A 100 percent PDQ would equal the sum of each of these assigned factors multiplied by 1. As you will see on the spreadsheet, this number is always 7800.

The penetration numerator in this example is 2300. Study the spreadsheet and you will see that zones G, C, B and K, where we had 100 percent penetration, were assigned the full value of their factors (100, 200, 300 and 400). Zones D, F, H, and J, which only had 50 Percent penetration, were assigned 50 percent of their factors (500, 600, 700 and 800). Our numerator of 2300 divided by the constant denominator of 7800 yielded a PDQ of 29.49.

With each entry, the PDQ will change because of its dynamic nature. The system's beauty lies in this attribute, in fact, and allowing you to accurately evaluate the use of your sales space regardless of seasonality and departmental changes. The system also allows you to compare two stores with completely different layouts and traffic counts as regards how effectively each utilizes space. In addition, you can quite simply monitor the impact of any changes that you make to your current layout by repeating the process a short time after you complete those changes.

Of course, to draw any conclusions from two shoppers as in this small example would be a waste a time. I have done this simply for the sake of illustration. On the other hand, to draw conclusions from a day's worth of charted traffic is quite illuminating.

What follows is a copy of an actual report that we recently created for a customer.

Penetration and Dispersion Quotient (PDQ) is a measurement designed to help you evaluate traffic flow through your store's sales space. The first step taken to establish your store's PDQ was to chart your customer's pathways as they navigated your sales area.

The ideal PDQ is 100 (a perfect score). In reality, it is unlikely that any store will ever reach 100. To reach that perfect measurement every customer who came into the test store during the period of our research would have had to pass through each of 12 zones dividing that store's sales space. **Penetration, for the purpose of the PDQ, is the measurement of the percentage of the people who came into the store and then walked into a specific zone.**

A copy of your store's layout is included with this report. Please refer to the drawing of your store to help you understand the information outlined below.

Your store's PDQ during the test period was **25.96**. *For a point of comparison, the average PDQ for stores we have analyzed is 23.83. The median PDQ for these same stores is 31.36.*

The PDQ is computed by establishing the percentage of customers who passed through the twelve zones of your store during our information-gathering process. A store will often have 100 percent penetration into **at least one** of the twelve zones because the entrance door is located in one of the twelve zones. When a customer enters your store, he **must** pass through the zone that contains the door, and therefore, by default this zone will have 100 percent penetration. Of course, if there are multiple entrances, this consideration is not applicable.

Usually, however, there will be two or three additional zones that will score 100 percent penetration. These zones are often to the right of the entrance zone. Depending on a store's layout, the customer service area may have 100 percent penetration as well. These statistics are to be expected, but beyond these tendencies, the flow of traffic in the rest of a store is unpredictable. Customer flow is dependent upon product placement and adjacencies, lighting, floor design and communicative signage. Fortunately, all of these things are within your control.

Once the penetration percentage of each of the zones is established, the zones are resorted in descending order by the penetration number. The chart below shows your store's zones and corresponding customer penetration percentages in each zone sorted in descending order.

Zone	Penetration	Zone	Penetration	Zone	Penetration
C	100.0%	E	31.9%	H	23.6%
B	100.0%	D	26.4%	G	18.1%
F	44.4%	J	25.0%	L	16.7%
A	41.7%	I	23.6%	K	13.9%

The zones are then assigned multiplying factors based upon their ranking of penetration. In the chart that follows, you will see that the zones most penetrated are the ones assigned the least value. They win somewhat by default. People are already passing through those zones.

Your challenge is to move customers into the areas of your store that they are currently not shopping. Therefore, we have assigned higher challenge/reward factor to those zones. The multiplying factors are static, remaining constant from study to study at a value of 100 to 1200 per zone in increments of 100.

The zones, to which those values are assigned, however, will change from study to study depending upon the penetration numbers. Therefore, the report is valid for any store size and at any point of seasonality. The chart below shows the static multiplying factors and the assignment of those factors to your store's zones based upon the penetration that we charted during our study.

Zone	Factor	Zone	Factor	Zone	Factor
C	100	E	500	H	900
B	200	D	600	G	1000
F	300	J	700	L	1100
A	400	I	800	K	1200

The following chart shows the results of multiplying the static factors by the dynamic penetration percentages correlated to the 12 zones of your store. The columns headed **Result** are the outcomes of those computations.

%	Factor	Result	%	Factor	Result	%	Factor	Result
100.0	100	100.0	31.9	500	159.72	23,6	900	212.50
100.0	200	200.0	26.4	600	158.33	18.1	1000	180.56
44.4	300	133.33	25.0	700	175.00	16.7	1100	183.33
41.7	400	166.67	23.6	800	188.89	13.9	1200	166.67

The total of these factors in your store was 2025.00, which becomes the numerator for figuring your stores PDQ. The denominator is always the same for every store, any size, and any location. The denominator is ascertained by multiplying every factor available for every zone by 100 percent. This is the number that would be indicated if every customer who came into your store during our study had walked into every zone of your store. This number is **always** 7800. Therefore, your PDQ of 25.96 was computed by dividing 2025.00 (your store's numerator) by 7800.

The higher your PDQ, the harder it will be to improve upon. The equations are designed that way. The beauty of the system, however, lies in its dynamic nature. This quality means that, after quite dramatic or even subtle changes to your store's layout or product placement, the system will level the field during its next use and give you an unbiased objective assessment of your improvement. Therefore, this valuable test should be done regularly.

Repeated PDQ testing is also a great way to monitor the effectiveness of your communication pieces. The impact of new communicative signage or accent lighting, for example, can be readily monitored.

During this study, we charted the courses of 72 people. Just like any other type of statistical analysis, the larger the studied group the more reliable the information. We have found that, if we study the flow of 100 customers within a store, we have obtained very reliable data. Your study did not meet that requirement. Therefore, you should probably repeat, the study in the near future.

Please notice that zones A, B, C and D, on the drawing of your store, comprise the front one-third of sales space. Your store achieved an average PDQ of 67.0 percent in this section. The middle one-third of your store (sections E, F, G, and H) and the back one-third of your store (sections I, J, K, and L) realized penetration rates of 29.5 percent and 19.8 percent respectively. This number is derived from totaling the penetration rate of the four zones of the target one-third of the sales space and dividing by four.

It is always harder to move people further back into a store. This is a job for creative layout, lighting, product placement and communicative signage. Focus on these factors will improve your store's PDQ; it will be well worth your effort and will reward you with increased sales.
Using the same type of analysis and the same equation, let's take a look at how your store performed mirrored right to left. The left-hand side of the sales space (sections A, B, E, F, I and J) produced a 44.4 percent penetration rate. The right side (sections C, D, G, H, K and

L) penetration rate was 33.1 percent. There is an 11.3 percent differential in the performance of side contrasted against side, which is within the 15-point range that we consider normal and have observed in a number of stores.

To reiterate, your store's PDQ is 25.96. The average PDQ that we have observed in our studies is 23.83. The median is 31.36. Although those numbers give you interesting points of comparison, the real benefit comes from contrasting your current number against future results. Improve your PDQ and you will improve your store's productivity.

If you have any questions or comments about the process or these results, please contact me so that we may discuss them.

Thanks for your participation.

Phil Mitchell
phil@philiphmitchell.com
Discovery-Based Retail

As you can see from the results of this report, this store is functioning as if it were a much *smaller* store simply because traffic is not flowing well throughout its floor space.

Establishing a store's PDQ is an excellent way to evaluate the need for change in an existing floor plan. It will help you identify the depth of your customers' penetration into your store, and it will quite clearly spell out the distribution of traffic through your store's sales space.

Chapter 4: Points to Remember

1. You communicate to your customers through the physical and environmental attributes of your store.
2. The layout of your store communicates where you want your customers to travel.
3. Deeper penetration into a store correlates with longer shop time, which in turn usually correlates with increased ticket size.
4. Before you can undertake a redesign of your current floor space, it makes sense to discover the upsides and the downsides of its current layout.
5. The best way to evaluate traffic flow in your store is by measuring your stores PDQ

Chapter 4: Action Steps

1. Divide a drawing of your store's existing sales floor space and into 12 equal-sized zones. The zones can be either 4 sections wide and 3 sections deep or 3 sections wide and 4 sections deep (this is dictated by the store's overall profile). If your store's space is irregular, try to divide the space as evenly as possible, but the division must be into 12 zones.
2. Using copies of this drawing, chart the flow of customers through your store for a day. We have found using a pen with four different colors of ink an effective way to provide distinction.
3. After you have charted traffic throughout your store (at least 100 people is best), use the formula in this chapter to figure your store's PDQ. If you want to ease the process, an Excel spreadsheet that will compute the PDQ is available on our website at www.discoverdbr. com.

DISCOVERING: A BETTER FLOOR PLAN DESIGN

After we have gathered the penetration statistics for a store's layout, we then examine its current layout in regard to the various zones to see what conclusions we might draw from the information. For example, we note the impact of the location of the cash wrap or customer service areas on the movement of people. We also determine which departments or gondolas are shopped most frequently and which are shopped least frequently.

Further, we do an extensive lighting analysis of the store to determine if that information correlates with movement into the various zones and with traffic overall. Lighting will be discussed to greater depth in a subsequent chapter.

Although the drawing on page 73 represents a hypothetical store, it is typical of some old and tired concepts. This floor plan, in fact, has few redeeming qualities, but nevertheless, it is an example of the type of floor plans that we encounter on a regular basis.

The one bright spot that we might point to in this plan is the fact that the "decompression zone" has been respected. The decompression zone, a term coined by Paco Underhill, refers to a 10' area inside the front door that is left relatively void of displays. This is the area where the customer adjusts to his new environment and makes his first assessment of your store. In short, the customer needs the uninterrupted area to transition into your world.

If you display merchandise, store shopping carts, or place signage in this area, you are likely to receive very little financial return for your efforts. Although the natural tendency may be to bombard customers with merchandise and communication pieces from the moment they enter the store, this is counter-productive in the decompression zone because the customer is busy making decisions regarding their path and objectives.

However, as I noted previously, this store design has few redeeming qualities beyond the decompression zone. For example, the entrance doors are at the bottom of the drawing, and the doors in the rear of the store exit into the lumber area. The dashed rectangles on both sides of the store near the front door represent areas where this imaginary lumber retailer showcases door and window displays, products that are a big part of his business. Consequently, the retailer feels that they need to be featured.

He's right, of course. These products do need to be featured. Windows and doors are a big part of most lumber retailers' businesses. However, there are far better locations within the store to address this need.

When designing floor plans, we strive to maximize the "feel" of the store size. In other words, we try to make the store look as big as it can look so that the customer feels that the retail space goes on and on, offering them more than other retailers that carry the same products. One of the ways to do this is to move the extreme-height displays, such as those for doors and windows, to locations nearer the walls and further back in the store.

The overall floor space represented by this hypothetical plan is in fact not large, but the point is that, if you were to walk into this store as it is presently laid out, you would feel that the retail space was even smaller and more confined than is actually the case. Upon entering this store, you might even describe your feeling as claustrophobic. It's easy to understand why. Although the decompression zone is uninterrupted, the customer service area appears forbidding, much like a wall or a barrier. This area communicates to entering customers that the counter is a good place to stop, and consequently, most people would indeed stop right here.

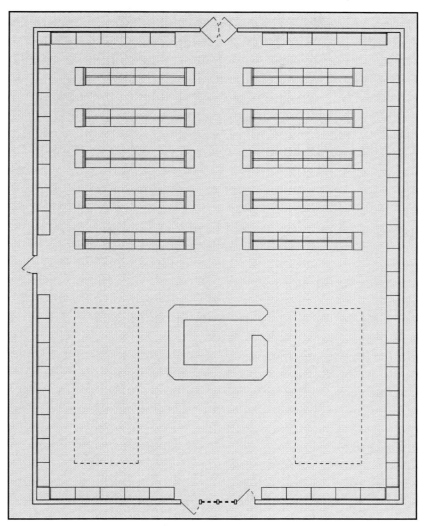

Couple the barrier-like customer service counter with the height and bulk presented by the adjacent window and door display areas, and you can see why a customer might feel as if he had to run the gauntlet just to shop the areas in the back of the store.

In fact, the layout of the store on the this page is such that it creates the feel of an auto-parts store, where the customer waits on a stool at the counter while the clerk fetches the parts from the shelves in back. The main problem with this scenario, of course, is that it stifles the perusal of associated or new items, and so limits the chances for impulse sales.

There are many floor plans that would improve the current layout. Consider this one:

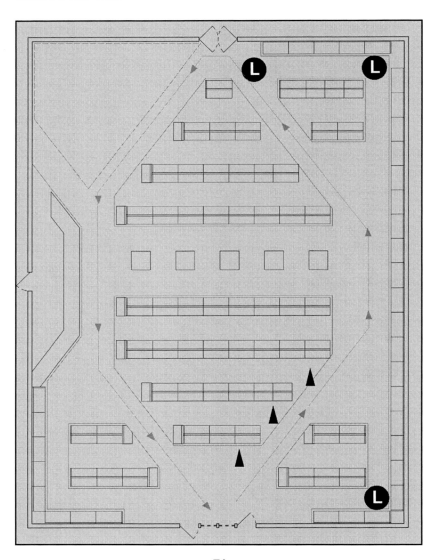

This layout would create better traffic flow. You will notice that the barrier of the cash wrap has been removed, and instead, the customer service area sits at the midpoint, along the left wall as you enter the store. Notice also that we have preserved the decompression zone.

The *current* floor plan would tend to draw people to the customer service counter, and once they had been waited on, most often their traffic pattern would then take them right back out the front door. We want to shake that traffic tendency up completely. Consequently, the new floor plan encourages a whirlpool-like traffic *flow*.

The term "flow" is often used to describe the movement of people, and the metaphor is apt. If you heard the word "flow" outside a retail context, you would probably associate it with liquid. If you imagine moving people through your store much as you would control the flow of liquid moving in an enclosed area, a tub perhaps, it will help you understand how to best facilitate the movement of people.

Anyone who has ever been in a shopping mall during the Christmas season and found himself in an aisle moving against the flow of people can appreciate the forces in operation. Think of the flow of water in a whirlpool, how its motion is almost self-generating once it gets started. This floor plan would encourage that same type of self-generating movement within this store, a powerful force moving through the sales space.

Upon entering a store, most customers will turn to the right. This phenomenon is not necessarily logical but it is statistically irrefutable. Paco Underhill has been credited with labeling this tendency the "invariant right." Underhill, in fact, states that as many as nine out of ten people move in that direction when given the opportunity.

Go back and take another look at the new floor plan. We have recommended three points of feature lighting, which are represented by the black circles with the white Ls on them. The traffic will tend to flow as directed by the angle of our floor design. The upward cascading angle draws people to a midway point on the right wall, which of course is in keeping with the customer's natural movement tendencies. He feels comfortable because the direction we are encouraging him to move is the direction in which he wants to move. We are, after all, only enforcing the invariant right.

The light in the front right-hand corner will have a tendency to pull customers' eyes in that direction. People gravitate to light. Without the feature lighting in the front right-hand corner, that area might go untraveled for the most part. The items featured in this spotlighted corner must also be attractive and colorful. We want people to shop this corner just as we want them to shop the rest of our store.

You can probably sense now that what we are doing is using the elements that we have *discovered* to maximize the potential of the store. We have created an atmosphere where we communicate that the customer *should* follow his natural tendencies — he *should* move to his right.

Whether the customer turns directly to the right and to the corner or if he walks up the cascading aisle, he will start a whirlpool-like traffic pattern within the store. Study the drawing and you can see how we continue to guide him along on his journey.

Let's say, for the sake of discussion, that the customer turned sharply right and headed toward the lighted feature in the corner. From that perspective, when he looks deeper into the store he will see the second area of featured lighting and the new direction that we want him to travel. It is interesting to note that we are communicating to our customer with nothing more than layout and lighting. We are quite literally directing the path of his shopping experience.

The angles we have introduced create a more interesting atmosphere than straight ranks of gondolas lined up like toy soldiers. I have heard people observe, however, that angled gondolas eat up floor space; and in the case of truly angled gondolas (or in other words, gondolas that are not positioned parallel with the walls), this is certainly true.

However, if you study this layout you will notice that the gondolas are actually running parallel with each other and parallel with the walls. It is only their terminal points that create the illusion of angles. In this drawing, I have represented floor tape to further accentuate those angles. In real world projects, we have used the tape in some stores and at other times let the point of sight alone create the angled look.

How many feet of display space are lost in this type of design? Typically, none. In the two drawings that you've seen, in fact, here's how the display space sorted out.

	New	Lineal Feet	Old	Lineal Feet
Wall Sections	34 sections 4' wide	136	54 sections 4' wide	216
Island Sections (4')	106 sections 4' wide	424	80 sections 4' wide	320
Island Sections (3')	12 sections 3' wide	36	None	0
End Caps	12 sections 3' wide	36	20 sections 3' wide	60
TOTALS		629		596

There are two important considerations in this contrast. Even though we gained total *lineal* feet of gondola space, we lost lineal footage of wall display. So, depending on the height of the gondolas along the wall and the island units as well, it is possible that *square footage* of display was sacrificed. It would be impossible to know until we were working with actual specifications.

Further, you can see from the drawings and this mathematical summary that end caps were decreased, and although that loss is reflected in the total lineal feet, some storeowners cry out that they need *more* end caps.

However, the angled presentation that has been hypothetically presented could be modified to include more end caps, but we have observed that end caps many times become simply extensions of the sides that they terminate and can actually be counterproductive. In other words, they often contain 3 feet of merchandise that should have been on the side counters to which they are adjacent. If, on the other hand, you have a program in place that monitors end caps and insures that they are changed regularly, if they are maintained with the proper signage and presentation, then allowing for more end caps makes sense.

Discovery-Based Retail

Even though the end cap count is down in the new floor plan, however, I would suggest that there are actually more *featured* areas in this layout than the one with the additional end caps.

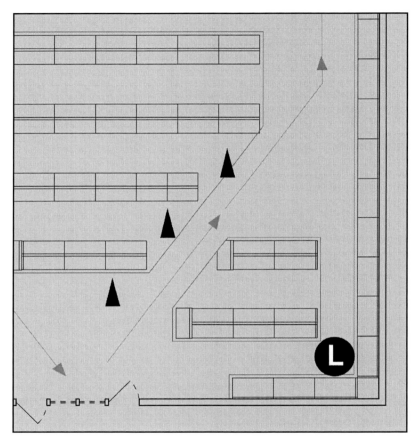

Imagine walking up the cascading front aisle of the new layout and try to visualize the amount of merchandise that would be revealed to you on your journey. I have drawn attention to the focal points with bold arrows in the insert above. You would be quite literally bombarded with exposure to merchandise. Now, keep in mind that this is just one aisle, one vantage point. We actually have the same type of product revelation occurring around the entire store, and this is true whether you are walking counter-clockwise as shown above or you do an about face and travel clockwise, against the "flow" within the store. Yes, John Denver, we would, indeed, fill up your senses in this retail operation layout.

Aside from the exposure of more merchandise from almost every vantage point, there are other positive effects that the new layout allows, including the customers' perception of the size of the store. Within the old layout, if a customer made it past the customer service desk and into the back of the store, he would have seen 16-foot gondola runs that sat perpendicular to an anemic power aisle. I characterize the power aisle as anemic because it was wide enough to introduce some space into the sales floor, and space is something that shoppers need in order to feel comfortable, but it was not wide enough to accommodate feature tables or feature stack-outs.

The new layout corrects this downside attribute of the current floor plan. The new feature aisle is set at an adequate width to accommodate either feature tables or stack outs. This new area would create interest, improve appearance and foster additional sales opportunities.

Another improvement to the perceived size of the store would lie in the extended length of the main gondola runs in the center of the store. The three longest runs, in fact, would be 32-feet long (8-4-foot sections).

Short gondola run lengths tend to fragment departmental layouts. The current 16-foot runs (4 sections of 4-foot gondolas) would dictate that categories be merchandised around corners and side to side. Although the new design would create *some* shorter runs, the new layout would also create a massive and expansive appearance in the center of the store. The long runs that would be situated perpendicular to the customer service area would invoke better vistas for the clerks working the sales floor as well, encouraging better communication and security in those areas.

At this point, it is important to mention gondola height, which is always a hot topic of discussion as I interact with dealers. The trend over the past few years has been toward taller gondolas, and this is particularly true of island fixtures. In stores where the ceiling height is sufficient, it is not uncommon to see 8-foot island fixtures. I have heard many arguments in favor of both the short and the high gondolas.

Remember this discussion is *primarily* about the island units, however, wall gondolas have historically been much taller. The higher wall units around the perimeter of the store are less invasive to the visual field than those in the center of the store.

OK, I'm going to take my politician's stance for a moment and say simply, "I feel strongly both ways." You're right, that's a cop-out. And after we discuss some pros and cons, I'll weigh in with a more biased opinion.

Some dealers refuse to consider taller gondolas simply because of the possible impact on shoplifting, but this is the argument with the dullest teeth. Some shoplifting will occur regardless of the height of the gondolas in your store. It's just a fact. In truth, if your gondolas were only 1-foot tall, those people who were going to steal from you would find a way to do it anyway.

There are locations where shoplifting is of great concern, and I don't mean to minimize that fact, but it doesn't make sense to fixture your store based upon theft, either. There are other ways (through creative layout, for example) to position the areas of greatest security concern in such a fashion that they are readily scrutinized, and this procedure can be implemented regardless of gondola height.

If you use taller fixtures, however, it is important to increase the aisle width. Narrow aisles and tall island gondolas create a very enclosed atmosphere. In fact, when designing a floor plan, we use a minimum aisle width of 4 feet when using six-foot or shorter gondolas and a minimum 5-foot aisle width when using taller fixtures. It is a fact that, because of this design differential, I would place more shorter fixtures in a store. That statement begs the question, "Do you achieve any more display area then?" The answer, of course, depends on the particular layout and the difference in the gondola heights in question. My only point is that, given the need for wider aisles when using taller fixtures, gaining display space is not guaranteed.

Increased aisle width when using taller fixtures is important not only for the feel of the aisles but also for adequate lighting. It is a matter of dispersion. Consider the beam of a flashlight. It travels quite well in the direction that it is pointed, but place a card or book in the line of its beam, and you block the light. The light will *not* reorganize and move around the obstacle. Duh!

Your display gondolas are like that book and your light fixtures are like the flashlight; the light will not simply reroute and go around the taller fixtures. The nearer the ceiling height to the top of the fixture, the more light flow is impeded. Light is critical in a store, and as the Baby Boomers continue to age, the more important the consideration of light should be to those trying to sell to members of this demographic.

But taller fixtures offer some advantages as well. It is true that you're already heating and lighting the area that taller gondolas would occupy. Doesn't it make sense to use that space? Just a few years ago the average inventory per square foot in a hardware store was in the low $30 range. The latest figures sited in the NRHA "Cost of Doing Business Study" placed this figure at the mid-to-upper $40 range.

Of course, some of this differential is simply the product of inflation, but dealers are also obviously trying to cram more products into the same amount of sales space in an effort to increase sales per square foot, and taller gondolas certainly aid in this effort.

There are other considerations to gondola height, of course, including the shopability and signage issues inherent to the taller displays. The debate has raged for a while now, and I certainly won't lay it to rest in this discussion.

I told you that I would express my *personal* opinion, and here it is. My recommendation would depend on the situation, of course, but I lean toward encouraging the use of 5-feet-6-inch or 6-foot fixtures. I have designed stores that used higher units, and personally, I just don't like what it does to the feel of a store.

As I have noted, people judge their shopping experience by their interpretation of the feel of your store, a mental composite that they construct based upon the impression that your store leaves on their senses: how it looks and sounds and smells to them. How do they feel when they're in it?

A store with tall gondolas has a different feel, one that I would characterize as more divided and less warm. So, in summary on the point of gondola height, I would simply say that you must let the situation dictate the decision.

This may sound like a political two-step, but store design is part science and part art. A store design that appeals to one storeowner may not appeal to another. However, I would encourage you to remember that your store's sales floor design is one powerful way that you communicate with your customers. It is a way to make customers feel welcomed into your store, a way to guide them through your store, and a way to fill up their senses while they are in your store. And a sales space design and presentation that is unique and interesting is an important way to separate yourself from your competitors.

Chapter 5: Points to Remember

1. The "decompression zone" is the area at the entrance of a store that is left virtually void of merchandise and store fixtures. It is an area that allows a consumer to adjust to your store's environment.
2. A good store design will maximize the perceived size of a store.
3. By placing the taller components of a store's display on the outside perimeter walls, a store takes on a larger look because of improved vistas.
4. The law of the "invariant right" says that people have a natural tendency to move to their right upon entering a store. Keep this in mind when assessing a new store plan.
5. The movement of customers can be guided by light, signage and fixture placement.
6. Gondolas running parallel to walls are an effective use of space.
7. Longer gondola runs improve perceived store size.
8. Taller fixtures require wider aisles.

Chapter 5: Action Steps

1. Walk through your store and consider the things that you have learned in this chapter. How does your store design embrace the "decompression zone" and the "invariant right"?
2. Would your store look bigger if the "eye barriers" were moved to the outside walls and the center of the store was more visually open?
3. Consider how long it has been since you have changed your floor plan. If it has been longer than four or five years, make contact with a floor plan designer and start the redesign process.

Chapter 6

DISCOVERING: IMPROVED LIGHTING AND COMMUNICATION

I have heard strange tales about the lighting practices of a small-town hardware store near where I grew up. Apparently, Francis, the store's proprietor, would regularly follow her customers from aisle to aisle, switching on and off the lights by pulling the strings attached to the various porcelain light holders suspended from the store's low, wooden ceiling. I guess she had mastered dynamic-feature lighting years before her time.

This would have taken place many decades ago now, but I still go into stores where the ambient lighting level is not much better than it probably was in Francis' store. No doubt Francis felt she was controlling expenses, and in an extreme way, she was only doing what store managers have always done: She was making a decision about an expense and taking action to support her decision.

During the time in which Francis operated, people didn't have a lot of retail choices. People were not as mobile as they are today and, in fact, her actions may not have seemed strange in the small community within which she operated. I can only speculate, of course, but Francis's store was in business for many years. Perhaps Francis just didn't understand how lighting moves and motivates people.

How important is good lighting within a store today? It's crucial and becoming more important with each passing year. Why is it becoming more important? The answer lies in the aging Baby Boomers — those of us born between 1946 and 1964.

We baby boomers are a large group that is only getting bigger. Consider this: Every 7 seconds another person from this age group turns 50. The number of people over the age of 50 increases 56 percent per year and will until 2011. Boomers are the largest spending group—$900 billion a year—and will control the vast majority of the nation's wealth within the next 20 years. (5)

Given those staggering statistics, here is the scoop for retailers as regards lighting: Try as we may, we Boomers cannot hold off the inevitable aging process, and unfortunately part of the aging process is deteriorating eyesight. It is simply harder for us to see in low-light environments than it was a few years ago.

Remember, we talked about the many ways in which you communicate to your potential customers. With the tremendous number of Baby Boomers and the immense amount of spending that they control, it makes sense to send a clear message to the members of this demographic that you want them in your store. Obviously, one way to communicate that message to them is by creating an environment in which they can easily see as they shop.

When we are helping store managers plan strategies for improving their store's performance, we use a digital light meter to measure ambient light levels from zone to zone within the store. If we are conducting a Penetration and Dispersion Quotient analysis, we look for a correlation between the movement of people within the store and the variant light levels from zone to zone. There often is just such a correlation.

But how much light is enough? Let's turn to some lighting experts for that information. The Solux Company specializes in creating lighting that mimics natural daylight. (6)

SoLux, a New York-based company, has an impressive list of clients, including the Van Gogh Museum in the Netherlands, Carnegie Museum in Pittsburgh, PA, and Memorial Art Gallery in Rochester, NY. Solux has also done extensive work in the realm of retail lighting,— consider this quote from its website: "The number of foot-candles required for reading and displaying items in a retail store is between 75 and 150 foot-candles [fc]".

I thought that it might be interesting to measure the light levels in a few stores, many of which will no doubt be familiar to you. I took the light meter that our company uses to Home Depot, Menard's, Lowe's and Sam's Club. These light levels are not necessarily representative of every store in each of the respective chains, but rather in the stores located near my home.

Two columns of the following chart represent the highest and lowest levels of lighting recorded (by fc) in each of the stores. The third column is simply an average of those two numbers and is listed only for a single-number point of reference.

Store	Lowest Level	Highest Level	Average
Menard's	51	169	110
Home Depot	30	174	102
Sam's Club	34	134	84
Lowe's	20	122	71

I would guess that, if I did this test in another set of the same brand stores, the results would be different. One important thing to observe, however, is that all of these chains consider lighting in their stores of great importance. If hardware is your business, you are competing against these stores.

Anecdotally, I will mention that my wife accompanied me on this odyssey. Upon entering the Lowe's store, she made the comment that this store "felt darker, more drab." Her statement hit home with me in two respects: first, that she associated the darker atmosphere with *drab* and, second, how she made the statement — the store *felt* darker. I want to emphasize again that the differences between stores in such environmental aspects as lighting are in perception and how a store *feels*.

OK, so all of this talk about foot-candles is fine, but what is a foot-candle anyway? Fortunately, I was lucky enough to find this picture of one:

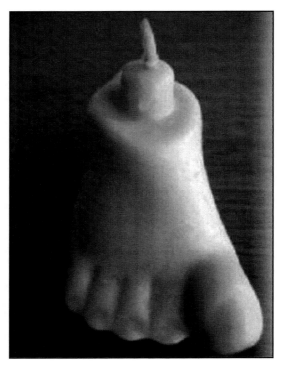

OK, it's just a joke. Take a deep breath. There you go. It's going to be OK.

GE used the wax candle in this picture as a promotional piece in the 1960s and, according to Wikipedia (the source of this picture), the sole of the foot candle has a message on it that reads, "GE makes the difference in light!"(7)

But alas, I digress. Back to the question at hand: What is a foot-candle? A foot-candle (again, abbreviated fc) is actually an old English measurement and one of the oldest measures of light. It is defined as *the amount of light cast by a standardized candle onto a one square foot surface from a distance of one foot.*

At the time the term was coined, using a candle for a standard illumination measurement made perfect sense. Candles, afterall, were a primary source of lighting and often used for reading.

Although the fc is still used extensively today, the International System unit of measurement for illumination is the Klux, which stands for kilo lux, or 1,000 lux. A lux (lx) is equal to one lumen per square meter. A fc is one lumen as well, but per square foot.

Therefore, if the same amount of light that illuminated one square foot to 1 fc was cast upon one square meter, it would illuminate roughly ten times more area and be only about 1/10 as bright. It would take roughly 10 lumens to light a square meter to the equivalent light level of one square foot lit to l fc.

Most digital light meters readily switch from lux to fc, but if you're one of those who wants the exact formula, here it is: 1fc = 10.75 lux.

OK, so what does all of this really mean to you as a storeowner or manager? Only this: Your store should have adequate ambient lighting to make your merchandise easily shopped and the information on its packaging easily read. This will require ambient lighting in the range of 75-150 fc.

The lumen capacity of light fixtures decreases over time, which is another aspect of lighting that is not readily recognized. There are actually two reasons for this decline in output: age and dirt accumulation. Consider the charts that follow provided courtesy of E Source Companies (8):

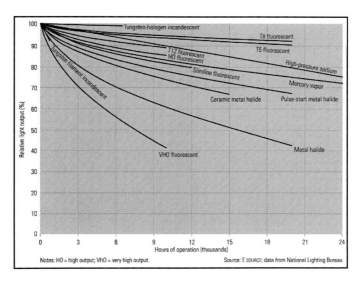

The chart above shows the percentage of lumen level decline over time with various light types.

The second chart illustrates the luminaire dirt depreciation (LDD) levels over a 3-year period, and charts the progress from a clean environment to an environment that has not been cleaned for 36 months. The last chart shows the percentages used to calculate LDD in environments that do qualify as "clean" environments (and let's hope all of our stores fall in this group).

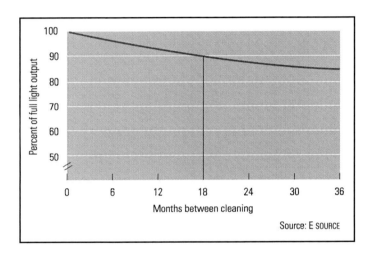

Source: E SOURCE

LDD factors		
	18 months since last cleaning	36 months since last cleaning
Fixture: open, unventilated, direct Environment: clean	0.92	.089
Fixture: open, unventilated, indirect Environment: moderate	0.76	.067
Fixture: other types, semi-indirect Environment: dirty	0.65	.048

These charts and some simple multiplication will reveal that what may have been an adequately lighted environment two or three years ago would not necessarily be that way today.

Recently, we had the chance to test these facts while working with a customer. We took light readings in conjunction with a Penetration and Dispersion Quotient analysis and found that three of the 12 sections of his store averaging 35-40 fc of illumination. After switching-out his 3-year-old bulbs, the light levels tested at a little over 50 fc. Of course, the difference was much more than merely a reading on a meter. It was very visually noticeable.

Obviously, the color and finish of the floor, the color of the fixtures, walls and signage also enter into the lighting equation for your store. There has been a tendency of late to leave concrete floors their natural gray color, finishing them only with sealer. Although this is obviously a cost-cutting measure, perhaps more consideration needs to be given to how the floor affects the overall lighting of a store and how the lighting will affect the store's performance in years to come.

Again, lighting has an impact on the *feel* of your store. Good lighting not only creates an environment that your customers will want to be in, but also provides a better working environment for you and your employees. This fact alone may be more important than you immediately realize.

I make this statement because of the the prominence of a *relatively* new psychological diagnosis called S.A.D., or seasonal affective disorder. Although the relationship of one's mood to one's exposure to light was first described in the 6th century, according to Wikiipedia, S.A.D. was not defined until much more recently.

According to Wikipedia, Norman E. Rosenthal, MD first proposed the diagnosis of seasonal affective disorder in 1984 when he: "became muggish during the winter after moving from sunny South Africa to New York. [and] He started experimenting with increasing exposure to artificial light and found this made a difference."(10)

I'm not suggesting that you use your store's sales floor as a treatment center for S.A.D., but rather, that the lighting within your store affects your mood, your employees' moods, and most importantly, your customers' moods.

I should note that the comments that I have made regarding lighting thus far apply to what I call a basic retail environment, which is how I would characterize a typical hardware store. Hardware stores usually have a standard product offering and a value-equation feel. They often have fairly high traffic and encourage self-service.

If you want to create a more upscale feel to your store and you feature specific products, then it makes sense to use a lower level of ambient light and to rely on accent lighting to help "paint" your environment to convey the appropriate message.

Although my background is in the hardware and variety store business, I have recently worked with some gift retailers. High ambient light would have been out of place in those stores. Further, higher ambient lighting would not have provided these stores' products with an upscale appearance, which is necessary to propel this type of niche business.

We have come full circle to what the lighting within a store communicates. In the case of the two gift stores that I just mentioned, the lower ambient lighting and increased use of accent lighting communicate the fact that the gifts in these stores are high in quality. Because of the environment that is created by this type of lighting treatment, the customer perceives that they can expect a degree of excellence from the items they purchase.

Here are a few final thoughts on lighting. Figure out exactly what you want to communicate to your ideal customers. Remember that you can use accent lighting to guide people through your sales space. Remember also that accent lighting can upscale a lower ambient light level environment, but bear in mind that everything is relative and if you accent everything, you have actually accented nothing.

We elected to cover lighting and signage in the same chapter because the two elements, lighting and décor, complement one another. When used in conjunction with accent lighting, signage can stand out. In the vernacular of the trade, it can really "pop," emphasizing the communication pieces.

Signage basically falls into three groups: decorative, adding eye-pleasing color; informational; or directional, providing guidance. Obviously, which type, and how much of each type, you should use is dependent upon the message that you want to communicate to your customers.

Oh no, you might be thinking, there he goes again, talking about communication with the customer. Enough already! I'm sorry to say that I probably won't stop! *Remember, there is nothing more important than successful communication with your customers.*

Good signage directs your customer's path through your store (remember the P.D.Q!), and good signage draws your customer's attention to the value that you bring to them. Good signage conveys project ideas and communicates *changes* within your store. In fact, if you change everything about your store and tell nobody, you have really changed nothing. Remember the three magic words: communicate, communicate, communicate!

Let's take a look at each of the three types of signs individually, starting with signs that add eye-pleasing color. These types of communication pieces include the lifestyle signs that have become more popular in recent years. Lifestyle signs usually depict vibrant, healthy and attractive people doing things that all of us would like to do. Sometimes the images are still-lifes, and feature perhaps a deck or swimming pool that would appeal to most of us. These signs typically feature near-photo quality images on vinyl banners, gator foam or other more rigid substrates.

What is the motivation for placing this type of signage in a retail environment? Here are some of the reasons:

1. To add color
2. To brighten the environment
3. To create a mood or "feel"
4. To communicate departmental division
5. To suggest projects

These signs, if done tastefully and in moderation, give an upscale appearance to a store's décor. Remember that the point of decoration is to *complement* the product offering, not upstage it. When the signage is overwhelming and distracting, it defeats the purpose for which it was intended.

The second type of sign is informational. This type of signage is not normally ornate, but rather, more purpose-specific in design. This type of signage conveys:

1. Pricing
2. Competitive pricing policies
3. Warranty Information
4. Hours of Operation
5. Mottos or policies

Although these signs can add color to an environment as well, they are primarily functional. Once again, however, notice that their function is communication.

The third type of signage is directional. Although the name for this type of sign is fairly self-decriptive, the group would include:

1. Departmental location signs
2. Product location signs
3. Customer service and checkout signs

These signs, particularly the departmental location signs, should be clearly visible across the store. When clerks are not available or when the customer would rather not ask, the departmental signs direct the customer to the position in space of specific departments. The product location signs further triangulate the position in space for individual products. If these signs all work together in a visible and appealing way, the customer can zone-in on what they are looking for. Make sure that these signs are clearly visible from the the entrance and main aisle of the store. Based upon our recommendation, a store recently staggered and turned their aisle directive signs 45 degrees. The improvement was dramatic while costing the store virtually nothing to implement.

Many franchise stores, or stores that belong to buying groups, have the option of participating in the identification packages that their franchise makes available to them. That said, some of the best looking individually owned stores that I have seen have "done their own thing." Although this might involve more upfront effort, and probably more cost, the distinction that these stores have accomplished for themselves pays for itself many times over.

Here's a point of alarm, however. The environment created by any signage and décor package needs to be updated periodically. It is just the nature of the beast. I have been in stores that were decorated ten years ago with what were then the state-of-the-art signage and graphics packages. Today, these stores look, as you would expect, old and tired.

Change is necessary in layout, signage and décor. Remember, you are communicating to your customers that you want your store to be interesting to them even though (and perhaps, especially if) they have shopped with you for a long period of time.

Chapter 6: Points to Remember

1. Lighting is important to a store's success, and it is becoming increasingly important because of the aging Baby Boomer population.
2. Lighting is communication with your customer.
3. Typical self-service retail environments require 75-150 fc.
4. Lighting guides traffic.
5. Lighting creates interest.
6. Lighting accents areas and products.
7. Lighting fixtures lose luminescence and become dirty over time, which causes the quality of light to deteriorate.
8. Interior signage adds color and interest.
9. Interior signage guides and directs traffic.
10. Interior signage communicates pricing and policies.

Chapter 6: Action Steps

1. Using a drawing of your store's current floor plan, divide the sales area into twelve equal parts..
2. Using a light meter, record the highest and lowest fc rating in each of the twelve zones.
3. Consider what you are trying to communicate to your ideal customer and determine if the light levels that you have recorded are in balance with that message.
4. If you find that you need to increase the light level in your store, start by cleaning the bulbs and fixtures, and then remeasure the fc level.
5. If after cleaning the fixtures and bulbs you find the light levels are still below a level that adequately communicates the message that you want to send to your customers, develop a strategy to address this concern.
6. Count the signs within your décor package and categorize each one into one of the three signage group types. Name them:
   a. Decorative
   b. Informational
   c. Directional
7. Once again, considering your ideal customer, objectively assess whether the signs are adequate in number, message and freshness to communicate what you want to convey.

Chapter 7

DISCOVERING: THE MEANING
OF CUSTOMER SERVICE

In the retail genre of non-fiction, no subject is written about more often than customer service. For that reason, I actually thought about avoiding the topic and leaving it for others to cover. However, after extensive discussion, I realized that even though it has already been viewed from many perspectives, to simply omit it would be an error of judgement. As a merchant, great customer service is the point of all your customer interactions, and thus is of paramount importance.

When the big box behemoths started slaying small stores all around the country, the universal battle cry from the independents who competed against them was "we will outservice them" and "people will come to us for what we know." Thankfully, even though these statements seem to have rather egotisical underpinnings, there is still an element of truth to them. However, as we mentioned in one of the earlier chapters of this book, those big box stores have large budgets for training and are obviously trying to close the customer service gap.

Perhaps we should consider the following question first: What is customer service? Better yet, what is *good* customer service and how does a store achieve it?

Let's start with a definition of customer service and frame it in relationship to a retail store. *Customer service is the sum of the acts and elements that allow consumers to receive what they need or desire from your retail establishment.*

But herein lies the problem. Consumers *expect* good customer service, and if consumers are *expecting* good customer service, they are expecting it from every store with which they do business. How then is it even possible to draw a point of differentiation between your business and others simply by providing what consumers already *expect* from every business?

Before we can answer that question, we need to understand that the term consumers includes all of us. And I don't know about you, but I don't always get what I expect from a retailer. The logical significance of that statement is that neither do consumers, as a group, always get what they expect.

My original contention was that consumers believe good customer service is an inherent right. Consumers are ready, willing and able to exchange their money for goods and or services, but those same consumers expect that good customer service is something that a merchant provides simply as a vehicle for the merchant's side of the transaction.

Customer service is thus not something that is "above and beyond," as we have lulled ourselves, or have been lulled by others, into thinking. In short, customers believe your company provides good customer service until you prove otherwise. And boy howdy, God help those who do!

Consider the following categories from the website www.mystrategicplan.com, a site that slots customers into profiles based upon these descriptions: (9)

1. Endorsers (5% of customer base) are customers who tell other people about your company. Typically, the new customer comes in as an endorser, which you should capitalize on.
2. Buyers (15% of the customer base) will continue to buy from you, often exclusively, but no longer aggressively endorse your company. Maybe an invoice was incorrect or a shipment was incomplete. If one negative incident moves your customer from endorser to buyer, it may take 15 positive incidents to get him or her back as an endorser.
3. Satisfied mutes (30% of the customer base) are customers who don't talk to you and to whom you don't talk. If you ask one of them how your business is doing, they answer, "Fine." And that's all you know.

4. Dissatisfied mutes (30% of the customer base) have migrated from the ranks of satisfied mutes, but you don't know it. That's because no one is talking to anyone else. At this stage, it will take 60 positive incidents to make this person an "endorser" again.

5. Grumblers (15% of the customer base) are customers you know. No matter what, you can't do anything right for them. They've experienced too many negative incidents. In essence, they have become "martyrs."

6. Complainers (5% of the customer base) are few in number, but this type of customer can be deadly. They make a point of telling everyone how badly your company has treated them. They are not your friends.

Allow me to reiterate a point, if you will. I made the comment that customers think that your store provides good customer service until you prove them wrong. Why would they think this? The better question would be: Why *wouldn't* they think this? Doesn't it make sense from every rational vantage point that you, as a merchant, would be taking care of the customers you depend upon for your livlihood? To think anything contrary would be irrational.

Now keep that thought in mind as we examine the first category defined above:

(1.) Endorsers are customers who tell other people about your company. Typically, the new customer comes in as an endorser, which you should capitalize on.

Why does she *come in* as an endorser? Simply put, because she is thinking rationally and expecting good customer service as a standard provision by the merchant in exchange for her business.

Perhaps the most alarming statement of the points made above is in point two: "If one negative incident moves your customer from endorser to buyer, it may take 15 positive incidents to get him or her back as an endorser."

Wow! I am not sure how this data was collected or how it was interpreted, but if that statement is true, it is staggering. As if that weren't bad enough, it gets even worse at other points along the scale: "At this stage [Dissatisfied Mutes], it will take 60 positive incidents to make this person an 'endorser' again."

This is a *big* problem. How many endorsers does your store have right now? How many customers do you have that are new enough that they have not once been dissatisfied with the service that your store provides?

Let me take you on a journey into a couple of personal experiences. I have lived in the town in which I reside for only two years, and I had no preconceived notions of where to do any type of business before I arrived. I recently bought a car from a dealership in town. I shopped at only one other place. I determined that, although the local guy was slightly higher, he was within the price range I considered to be a good trade off for keeping my business in town.

I was satisfied with the transaction, and when my friends asked me if I got a good deal, I responded, "Yeah, I felt like I got a good deal." Notice my choice of words reflected my feelings only and had no relationship to the strange benchmark we call reality.

OK, fast-forward about six months. I was having my car serviced at a local quick-lube business when the serviceman told me that he found a slight leak in the transmission. He told me that I should check with the dealer that I bought the car from because the warranty would probably cover it.

Acting on his advice, I checked with my dealer, who told me that, yes, indeed, the transmission would be warranted. My wife reminded me that, when I took the car in for repair, I should have them touch up the little paint ding that was on the side of the car when we took delivery. Our salesman had promised to have it fixed when he sold us the car.

"Why haven't they fixed it yet?" I asked her.

"I don't know," she said. "They were supposed to call us when the right guy came in to do it."

I was puzzled. We had forgotten about the ding and the promise (at least I had) and, apparently, even though he had assured us he would call, our salesman had forgotten about it as well.

I explained all of the details to the shop foreman, and he assured me that they would take care of the leak, send the car over to the body shop to have it touched up, and then give me a call so I could pick it up. I thought, "Man, am I lucky. The one guy who could touch up the ding must be working today."

I waited for a call, but it didn't come. I waited two days. Finally I called and asked if my car was done. The shop foreman said, "Didn't we call you?"

"Nope."

"Well," he said, "the car is over at the body shop. It should be done over there, but we had to order the part for the transmission."

"Can I pick it up and drive it while we're waiting for the part?"

"Sure, that'd be a good idea."

"Damned straight," I thought.

So I went to pick up my car at the body shop. The clerk greeted me warmly, made me feel comfortable entering his office, and then proceeded to explain to me that he was unaware that my car was supposed to be touched up.

"It's sitting right out there," I said, pointing to the car.

"Um, well I'll be," he said scratching his chin. "You know I wondered what that car was out there for."

I hung my head in exasperation as I listened to him call the service shop to try to determine where their communication had broken down.

"That explains it," he said, winking at me reassuringly as he finished his conversation.

He hung up the phone and began to explain. "Our part-time kid brought the car over. He didn't say anything about it. He just hung the keys in here." He reached around the corner and retrieved my keys from a hook on the wall. "We'll fix it when you bring your car back to get the transmission fixed. I made myself a note."

For some reason, I didn't feel assured.

About ten days later, I finally received a call from the dealership. My part was in, the clerk explained, and they would get me fixed right up.

When I picked the car up, the transmission was fixed and the paint nick was touched up. Did the car look good? Well, yes and no. The ding was gone, but a two foot radius around where the blemish had been was clean — bright white. The rest of the car reflected the grime of all the snowy days that we had just endured. If it hadn't been for the rest of the fiasco of this customer service experience, I probably wouldn't have even thought twice about them not washing the entire car after the touch up; but because of all of the other miscues, it kind of rubbed me the wrong way.

What is the point of this rambling? I heartily entered into the ranks of an endorser with this dealership. I was pleased with my first interaction with them. I told my friends that I "felt" like I got a good deal. Am I still an endorser? No! Will I buy another car from the dealership? I seriously doubt it. The fact is that I probably won't have enough interaction with them to recover my confidence in them.

OK, now contrast that experience against this one. When we completed our new home, we left one room unfinished, which was to be the room of our dreams — a home theater with an eight-foot screen, killer sound system, and plush reclining-style theater seats.

One day we found ourselves energized and my wife and I decided to undertake the project ourselves. After shopping for the theater furniture at several different places, we settled on a destination store in Kansas City about 35 miles from our home.

The day before the delivery was scheduled, I received a call explaining that I should expect delivery of the furniture the next day (which was the day delivery was originally scheduled) between 8 and 10 a.m. The call was from an automated system.

The next morning at about 8:10, the doorbell rang — the deliverymen had arrived. It had been snowing a lot, and consequently our driveway and yard were still a mess. I was somewhat hesitant to show the deliverymen where I wanted the seats. The site was in the basement, and I knew that it would be difficult for the men to get the furniture down there.

The foreman of the two-man crew had a thick accent that I guessed to be Jamaican.

"No problem, mon!" he said with a toothy grin. "How 'bout wes bring 'em through thot door?" He pointed to the sliding door at the back of the house.

"That would be great, but it would mean walking down the side of the house in the snow."

"No problem, mon!"

He and his partner made short work of bringing the six heavy pieces down the hill, around the house, and through the sliding walkout basement doors. They paid an extreme amount of attention to my desires and showed great respect for their duties.

But the story doesn't end there. My phone rang again at 10:05. It was another call from the furniture store, but this time it was real voice.

"Hello."

"May I speak to Phil Mitchell?"

"That's me."

"Mr. Mitchell, this is Mike with ******** ********* ****. I was checking to see if your furniture arrived within the 8 o'clock to 10 o'clock window that we promised you?"

"Yeah, it did!"

"Was the furniture right and did it work as you wanted?"

"Yes it was, and yes it did."

"Were our drivers courteous and helpful."

"Almost unbelievably so," I answered.

"Well, thanks for your business. We appreciate it."

You know what? They had already communicated with their actions that they appreciated my business. Mike's words were in harmony with the actions of the deliverymen.

This store did appreciate my business. Wow, was that refreshing! This is a huge store, and I'm willing to bet they continue to grow as long as they show their customers this level of service.

Perhaps the irony of these two disparate stories is this: The large (category killer-type) furniture store's service was unbelievably good. The local car dealer's customer service was, in my opinion, unacceptably poor. Remember the battle cry of the small independents: We will out service them? Don't look now folks, but it didn't happen in the cases just presented. Am I an endorser for the furniture store? You bet I am. They raised the bar to a high level and then took a flying leap and jumped above it. As regards the auto dealer in my hometown, I have joined the ranks of "dissatisfied mutes." I would bet that I am not alone.

So what should an independent business operator take from this? Should he be discouraged at the additional resources that the behemoth brought to play in the experiences I have described?

Well, I guess that's one way to react to it, but I think the better way, the more productive way, is to simply ask this question: What would have happened if the car dealer had all of his customer service ducks in a row? I would still be an endorser for his company. The size of the two companies was not the difference. The level of customer service was. Customer service systems and safeguards were simply not in place at the car dealership.

It's ironic and rather sad that the dollars this dealer spends on advertising will have no effect on those of us who have become his "Dissatisfied Mute" group, but rather, will probably only generate short-term endorsers who evolve into something else.

It's time to start thinking about customer service in a brand new way. It's time to take stock of the services you provide to your customers and evaluate those services in new and different ways. The services that you are providing, the same services that your consumers expect, must be done exceedingly well to avoid fallout (endorsers slipping down the scale), but moreover, to regain the support of those who have fallen from the endorser ranks.

The glass-half-empty guy might cry out, "If we've lost the endorser's support, what's the use?" To this I would answer: If nothing else, you can keep new customers as endorsers. Will you regain every dissatisfied mute? Probably not, but you don't know what strides you can make until you take your first step!"

Where do we start then? It's a great idea to chart all of the services that you provide to your customers under the umbrella of customer service. Below we have outlined a simple table to give you an idea how you might begin.

Service	Expected	Unexpected	Grade	Improvement
Checkout	x		B	Train checkers for improved speed
Gift Wrapping		x	B	Communicate this service with signage
Delivery	x		B	Train drivers on etiquette and efficiency
Coffee and Popcorn		x	B+	Make sure that all customers are invited to partake of treats
Design Assistance		x	A-	Advertise this obscure service more often

Start by listing all of the services you provide in the first column. It is important to list all of your services before you evaluate or grade them. After you have listed your services, consider whether your type of store normally offers them. If they are normal (and most will be), place a check in the box headed "expected," and if they are not offered as a matter of normal procedure in stores of your type, check the column headed "unexpected." You might more accurately characterize these services as innovative.

The next column is perhaps the most difficult because you have to divorce yourself emotionally from your store. You have to objectively evaluate the services and assign a grade to each you have listed. Remember to do this to both the expected and the unexpected services you offer. Devise your own grading system, but try to be consistent. It's probably a good idea to evaluate through hypercritical eyes. Your customers do!

Speaking of customers, you might also give them a copy of the services tables (minus the expected/unexpected columns) and ask them to grade your services and, if they're willing, to suggest improvements.

After *you* have assigned a grade to each of the services you offer, meet with your staff and share the information that you have compiled. This will yield a couple of positive results. It will let your staff know that you are placing a high degree of importance on customer service and they should as well. It will also allow your employees to become part of the solution to improve any anemic services that you uncover.

After you have thoroughly evaluated the services that you offer, it's a great idea to undertake the same type of evaluation of your competitors' services. Our company performs this function for our clients during the Competitor Contrast module. We have found this exercise to be very enlightening, and it serves as a great way to help determine how an unbiased consumer might view the differences between your store and your competitors' stores. I will talk more about this in a later chapter.

One advantage of using outside opinion for this type of evaluation is that the evaluators have no preconceived notions. Therefore, their evaluation is probably unbiased. Remember, your evaluation process may not make customer service strengths and shortcomings readily apparent. For example, we contrast hours of operation in our Competitor Contrast module.

But wait, you might say, what do store hours have to do with customer service? Remember our definition: "Customer service is the sum of the acts and elements that allow consumers to receive what they need or desire from your retail establishment." It's a lead-pipe cinch that, if your store is not open when it's convenient for me to shop, you will not meet my needs or desires for your products or services. Therefore, by our definition, your hours of operation must be compared against your competitors'.

By using our definition, you'll be examining your location, your parking, and every other element of your store that engages a customer or interfaces with her shopping experience. That is, every element of her shopping experience is, by our definition, customer service.

Remember my experiences with the furniture delivery and the post-sale car service. Customer service did not end at the sales counter, but rather, carried on until the conclusion of the transaction. In the case of the auto service, it meant that the customer service element of my initial purchase had no end. My desire for quality service extends over the entire course of my ownership of the car, or to quote Randy Travis, "Love without end, Amen!" (I don't know what made me do that!)

Does that mean that the chart that we started above should include things like location, parking, and hours of operation? Yes!

That's exactly the process that our company goes through when we do an examination of competitors for a client. All of these elements enter into a potential customer's decision about where he or she will shop and buy. All of these elements become bits and pieces of the impression that a potential customer has of your store.

If you're thinking that I'm getting carried away with all of this other stuff when I told you that I was going to talk customer service, I guess you're right. I am, that is, if you don't believe that it's a war out there. I am, that is, if you don't believe every store in the country is in a dogfight to attract and keep its customers. Well, on second thought, maybe I'm *not* getting carried away, after all.

I'll bet I know what you're thinking: "Will you stick a sock in it already about all the other stuff? Talk to me about customer service in the traditional sense, you know, my people helping my customers?"

OK, I'll make you a deal. I'll talk to you about clerks helping customers, if you'll promise to remember that it's only a small piece of customer service. You're right, of course. In the traditional sense, "customer service" probably conjures an image of a clerk showing a product, hopefully touting its virtues, and then perhaps even completing the sale at the cash register.

But then again, hopefully, you've already decided that this is not a *traditional* book on retail. I'll grant you, however, that to forego a discussion about this element of customer service would be unacceptable. So here we go.

When the effectiveness of a clerk is considered, there are two elements that should be weighed: ability to help and willingness to help. The first element is the *ability* of the clerk to help. This measurement would be the sum of the clerk's knowledge about the store — including layout, product locations, and policies and procedures — and, of course, its products. How familiar is he or she with the specific applications of the products in the area for which he or she is responsible?

As you can see, the elements in the *ability* side of our customer service evaluation are all achievable through training. If a person lacks knowledge on any of the elements mentioned to this point, training can help fill the void.

The second element of consideration is the clerk's *willingness* to help. When we are talking about a clerk's willingness to help, we are actually talking about attitude and work ethic. Although coaching and training may help change people's aptitudes, we are not convinced that attitude is as easily molded as knowledge. The elements that form attitude, as well as those that govern drive and desire, are much more deeply engrained in an individual's personality.

In his book *Good to Great,* Jim Collins made the observation that the companies that achieved greatness were often those that (I am paraphrasing here) decided who should be on the bus before they decided where the bus should be going. Mr. Collins' bus analogy showed that employees were the cornerstone of success for the companies he studied, and the same should hold for your company. (10)

We can study building location and attributes, traffic flow, and competitors. We can delve into statistics, matrixes and benchmarks, but in the final analysis, a retail store's success boils down to how customers *feel* about their shopping experience in that store. With that in mind, think about your employees right now. Think about the guy that you've tolerated simply because it was easier than the alternative, taking the time and effort to replace him.

You might counter, "Well, wait a second, old Fred has some good qualities, and he's always here.".

Yeah, so are germs!

I'll take your word about Fred — after all, I don't even know the guy — but ask yourself this question: Do all of my employees communicate the message that I want my customers to hear? Are they friendly and upbeat, courteous and knowledgeable? Do they make my customers *feel* good about their shopping experience?

We might as well dig a little deeper. After all, you're mad already. You didn't like what I said about Fred, not one little bit! So here's another point to ponder: How's *your* attitude?

You're the leader of the crew. Does your enthusiasm for what you're doing ignite enthusiasm in those around you? Enthusiasm, I am convinced, is contagious and will communicate more to your employees and your customers than your words ever will.

We once worked with a store where the owner/manager simply hated being at his place of business. Bill had worked long and hard hours for several years, and those tough times had taken a toll on him. Come to think of it, I'm not sure Bill *ever* liked dealing with his customers or employees. He confided to me one day that he thought he would be much happier if he were alone and driving his tractor, plowing his fields.

Everybody else would have been happier too. He wasn't fooling anybody. He was as out of place in his store as a catfish would be on a slab of hot-August asphalt. He was always complaining about his crew and their incompetence. Incompetence surrounded him, he said.

That doesn't surprise me. I don't suppose I would be at my best working around his cancerous mood, either.

Your store has an attitude. It's the sum of the attitudes of the individuals who man it, including you — nay, especially you! Your store's attitude is either positive and moves you closer to your performance goals, or it's negative and takes you, just as certainly, away from those goals.

Perhaps I sound eccentric about this topic, but please color me passionate instead. I have witnessed many managers trying to find answers to their store's problems, and in some cases, while they looked laboriously at every inch of the 3,000 square feet of their store, they failed to look at the small area between their ears — their *own* attitudes. Consequently, they never located their problem.

Never forget that you, as the leader of the store, set the tone for the attitude of the aggregate, and just as rationally as a surgeon will remove cancerous cells to save a life, so should you remove those unsalvageable employees whose caustic attitudes jeopardize the life of your business.

We have seen stores succeed in the most unlikely of locations and circumstances. We have also witnessed stores that have failed when all of the traditional barometers indicated smooth sailing. In short, never underestimate the importance of attitude in relationship to a business's success.

I'll never forget the day that I wandered into the grand opening of a Wal-Mart Super Center. I actually entered the store shortly before they opened their doors for business that day. This was shortly before Sam Walton passed away, but he was in attendance, passionately leading an enthusiastic group with this cheer: "Give me a W! Give me an A! Give me an L!" You get the picture.

I was awe-struck that day! It hit me like a lightning bolt! With all of the systems that this mega-company has in place to cover every conceivable facet of business, its founder still recognized that attitude was at the foundation of it all.

Thanks for the lesson, Sam.

Chapter 7: Points to Remember

1. Customer service is the sum of the acts and elements that allow consumers to receive what they need or desire from your retail establishment.
2. Although independents have hung their survival hats on the hook of customer service, *some* category killer stores are working arduously to achieve higher levels of customer service themselves, too.
3. Customers expect good customer service! If customer service is to be perceived as "value added," it must far exceed the norm for your industry.
4. Because new customers expect good customer service, they will assume you provide it until you prove to them otherwise.
5. An independent store does not have good customer service accidently. It is the product of procedure, policy and training.
6. Customer service goes far beyond a moment of dialogue between a customer and an employee. It also includes every other aspect of your operation that affects a shopper's experience in your store.
7. Customer service is not limited to those who directly interact with the customers. Every employee of the company contributes to a store's attitude and, therefore, contributes to its customer service.
8. A store's attitude can be the difference between success and failure.
9. The manager is the cornerstone of a store's attitude, and employees, whose attitudes are frequently a reflection of their boss's attitude, are the cornerstone of any excellent business.

Chapter 7: Action Steps

1. Schedule some quiet time and ponder all of the elements that you can think of that affect a customer's experience in your store.
2. Create a grade card like the example in this chapter. Divide the grade card into two sections. One section will involve the human interface element, and the other will involve all of the other elements that constitute a shopper's experience in your store. Remember to categorize these points as either expected or unexpected from your industry.
3. After you have created your list, let it simmer for a day or two. Schedule another meeting with yourself to analyze and grade your store on each of the elements you have listed.
4. Schedule a meeting with your staff and share the list that you have compiled, as well as the new definition of customer service.
5. Ask for their input regarding ways to improve the items you listed but did not assign an A grade.
6. Working with your employees, develop *systems* to insure that they and you are monitoring the items on your list and that the procedures for improvement are implemented consistently.
7. Go through a similar analysis of your competitors' services and interfaces. Objectively assess how they are providing better customer service than you are providing. Learn from them!

Chapter 8

DISCOVERING:
A SLOT FOR SUCCESS

As a boy, I once lamented to my father that I wished I could be as good at basketball as some of my friends. Skinny and gangly, I must have looked like the cartoon version of Ichabod Crane as I lumbered up and down the gymnasium floor.

Dad chuckled, thought for a moment, and then he said, "You know, the world just wouldn't work if we were all alike, son, or if we were all good at the same things. Your friends may be better than you are at basketball (he knew they were!), but there are things that you'll excel at. Learn what *those* things are and you'll be just fine."

I guess my dad was right. Throughout the years I've found some things that I can do pretty well. Not one of them, however, requires physical prowess. You might say that, as my life has evolved, I've found my slot.

Have you found your store's slot? Do you know what you do well and how you fit into the trade territory? Of course, just as I wished that I could be an athlete, it would be unrealistic for every storeowner to wish to dominate his market. It does mean, however, that every store manager should strive to operate his store within its slot of success.

The day that the importance of a store's slot really hit home with me was the day that we were doing a Penetration and Dispersion Quotient analysis for a 3,000-square-foot hardware store. As we reviewed the store's traffic flow information, we were puzzled. It seemed that every shopper went to her destination within the store, purchased her desired item, and then turned to leave. In a subsequent meeting with the store manager, he confirmed our immediate conclusion.

"Yeah, most of the people who come in are looking for something specific. They know what they want, and most of the time they know where to find it in my store. So, they come in, buy that item, and then they're out of here."

When we asked the store manager about his average transaction size, the figure that he quoted was, we thought, surprisingly low. After reviewing all of the data that the manager provided, we verified our conclusion that the store was actually a convenience store — *a convenience store that just happened to be selling hardware.*

Within the retail industry, people often banter about the term "convenience." This store was a hardware store, but if there are convenience stores that sell other items, doesn't it follow then that there are convenience hardware stores, indeed that convenience stores are a category in all other retail realms as well?

These thoughts raise a myriad of questions! If there are convenience stores, what are all of the other stores that are selling similar products called? Are all of the others the same, and if not, how do *they* differ? Are the other store slots better than the convenience group? If my store is functioning as a convenience store, should I strive to position it differently within my trade territory, and what would that take?

Our company has developed a classification system to identify a store's slot. This five-slot divisional description is valid across the retail spectrum. There are characteristics that are associated with each slot, and inherent opportunities and pitfalls accompany each. Understanding the slot within which your store operates can guide you in a variety of decisions.

Your Store's Slot of Success

Store Type	Destination Store	Regional Competitor	Convenience	Price Driven Niche	Product Driven Niche
Location	Provides own draw	Location important	Location way important	Location not as important	Location not as important
Building	Expansive	Moderate size	Smaller than regional competitors	Depends on featured products	Depends on featured products
Hours of Operation	Extended	Normal	Extended	Normal	Below Normal
Breadth of Merchandise	Very wide	Wide	Narrow	Narrow	Wide in narrow category
Depth of Selection	Vert deep	Normal	Shallow	Very deep	Normal
Pricing	Aggressive	Competitive	Margin focused	Aggressive	Margin focused
Average Ticket Size	Large	Moderate	Small	Depends on niche	Depends on niche
Margin	Short	Industry average	Should be higher than industry average	Short	Higher than industry average
Breadth of Appeal	Broad	Moderate	Narrow	Narrow	Narrow
Source of Appeal	Pricing, selection, entertainment	Location, selection	Convenience, easy in, easy out	Pricing	Broad selection in narrow categories
Independant Draw	High	Moderate	Low	Low	Low
Interaction With Customer	Low	High	Moderate	Moderate	High

The table above outlines some typical characteristics of the five store-slot types that we have identified, but let's take a look at the definition of each store's description before we discuss in-depth the pitfalls and opportunities that accompany them.

A *Destination Store* is just what the name implies. By virtue of its size, breadth of product offering, competitive pricing or entertainment value, a destination store will attract many customers, some driving considerable distances for their shopping experience. Robert Spector's wrote his book *Category Killers* about stores that fit in this slot. (11)

These stores are typically the largest of their type within the area they serve, and because of their retail pull, their geographical areas are quite large. In fact, one such store was recently built near where I live. Throwing out all of the ideas of locating near other stores in order to feed off their customer base, this store instead built on the other end of town. They seem to be doing just fine, thank you, because they are indeed a store that serves as a destination.

Destination stores appeal because of their assortment, their pricing or their entertainment value. Personal interaction with customers in these stores is not a high priority for the managers and staff.

Because destination stores operate in an ultra-competitive arena, prices are hot, but because of the buying power that these stores represent, negotiated costs allow margins to remain adequate to power their profitability.

When people frequent a destination store, their shopping carts are often loaded to the brim. These stores seem to be favored sources for projects and major purchases, and therefore, their average ticket size is large.

A *Regional Competitor* slotted store, on the other hand, will probably not attract customers from distant points. A regional competitor will rely on the retail pull of the community in which it is located.

However, regional competitors are considered competitive sources within their geographical area. This store type has a sizeable offering across a moderately wide spectrum of categories. Their hours of operation usually reflect those of similar store types within the trade territory.

The buffer distance separating a regional competitor from a destination store will have a huge effect on the success of this store type. The greater the distance of separation, the greater the likelihood the store will thrive.

Because this store type will have the ability to provide project sales, their average ticket size can be moderate to large. However, the need to compete with the destination stores, coupled with a lesser ability to negotiate prices, will mean the regional competitor must operate very carefully to maintain adequate margin.

A *Convenience Store* slotted operation is *almost* always smaller than a regional competitor. Because of its limited offering, a convenience store attracts shoppers who find the location of the store or the time spent to shop it easy and efficient. The convenience to cost ratio means that these shoppers will often just pick up a few things.

By virtue of this characteristic, the transaction size of a convenience store is smaller than that of a regional competitor. Therefore, the margins that a convenience store generates must be higher than the industry average in order to equate to profitability. In the truest sense of the description, this type of store may require more hours of operation to accommodate the convenience factor. Remember that the convenience factor must be analyzed from a customer's point of view and not from that of the store's staff.

Niche Stores fall into two distinct slots, either *product* driven or *price* driven. A product-driven niche store will feature extreme breadth of offering in a very narrow category.

For example, let us say that an employee of a destination store in the craft business, perhaps a Hobby Lobby, decides to open a hobby store of her own. Her chance of competing at the level of her former employer in a broad spectrum of categories is very slim indeed. More than likely, she would not have the name recognition or the resources to do so.

On the other hand, if she elected to open a store devoted to scrapbooking, for instance, provided the demographic characteristics of the area in which she operated supported the endeavor, and if she leveraged her wide-assortment offering with expertise and entertainment value in the form of workshops or group activities, she might well be successful. Her sales would pale in comparison to Hobby Lobby, but with adequate margin, she might meet her profitability goals. Of course, she would need to have a much wider offering in this specific category than did her former employer, but *only* in this category!

Now let's examine an example of a *Price-Driven Niche* store. Within the community in which I formerly resided, there was a lumberyard that

I would have characterized as a regional competitor in the lumber and hardware business.

At some point in time, however, the manager of this operation decided to try to "own" the narrow category of steel products. He wanted to be a major player within the category and he was successful. He bought huge quantities of steel products and sold through at the narrowest of margins.

Eventually, he had his own fleet of trucks to pick up the products at their source and, through this effort, he drove down his costs and the steel goods niche became profitable. If anyone for miles around had need for large quantities of steel posts, barbed wire, reinforcement bar, or any other associated steel products, they were probably aware of this store.

Would he have been successful if steel goods were his only business? I can't say for sure, of course, but I suspect he would have been successful given the time and resources to develop the niche. But perhaps the other parts of his business funded that luxury. I can only speculate.

But, if steel goods had been his only business, he would have been a price-driven niche slotted store. Price, after all, was his biggest claim to fame.

I have used this example to make another point: Although the word "slot" probably conjures an image of a constricted or clearly delineated description, the truth is that many stores straddle the lines represented in our chart.

If we could sit down with a box of crayons, I think that I could easily show you how the steel goods benefited the store in the example above; but because we're not together, I'm going to describe to you how I would use my Crayolas.

Let's say that we have three crayons: purple, red and blue. *Destination Store's* are purple, *Regional Competitors* are red, and both types of *Niche Stores* are blue.

Let's begin by filling in a few rectangles with red that represent our example lumberyard and his competitors. Each of these red rectangles represents a regional competitor. Now, in order to represent the price-driven niche characteristic of his steel products, we must color a stripe of blue onto the red rectangle that represents his store. But wait a second, something's happened. The blue strip that I colored doesn't look blue at all! Because it's blue on red, it actually looks more purple than blue.

Purple, you'll remember, is the color we designated for destination stores. In fact, if we were using watercolors instead of crayons, we would observe that the purple would slowly diffuse and would eventually cover more than the small band to which we applied the blue. So, with steel goods as a point of differentiation, this regional competitor store has actually taken on some of the characteristics of a destination store!

Use your imagination. The most important aspect of this discussion is that you need to have a clear vision of your store's slot, or how it fits into the operational arena within its community.

One might ask, is one store type inherently better than another? Well, define better. Under certain circumstances, a convenience store is the only type that has the potential for success. Will a convenience store's measurable success correlate with the money produced by a destination store? Of course not, but given identical circumstances, a destination store would not even be viable.

Should a convenience store strive to become a regional competitor? A storeowner in such a region should focus not on that, but rather, on identifying the slot that can maximize her potential for success given her realistic operational parameters. Ultimately, your only goal should be to become as profitable as you can. Trying to discover a store's slot always brings to mind the old saying "bloom where you are planted."

For example, if you operate as a convenience store, make sure that your retail prices are *high* enough to assure your existence. I have worked with store managers who actually felt guilty about raising margins, but to compare the prices of a convenience store against industry benchmarks can be misleading and fatal. If you are operating as a convenience store, you *must* maintain good margins. In fact, if you are not getting complaints about your prices, then perhaps you aren't priced high enough! We'll talk more about this in Chapter 14.

Of course, setting prices based upon your store's slot within the retail spectrum is just one action that can result from the Slot Discovery Process. The same information can guide your forecasts, advertising strategies, merchandise selection and even the environment that you create to communicate your positioning. If you have a clear understanding of how your store fits into the retail strata of its operational area, you will be much more able to convey that message to your customers.

When formulating a strategy regarding your store's slot, remember my story about the crayons. Red isn't necessarily red and blue isn't necessarily blue. A combination can create blends, and a blend can be your best strategy — but you do need a strategy! Be creative when looking at opportunities for your store. Then pick up your crayons and color your store a success!

Chapter 8: Points to Remember

1. A store operates primarily within one of five store-type slots
2. Any of those five slots presents unique challenges and opportunities.
3. No slot is fundamentally better than another, only different.
4. By identifying your store's slot, you can better formulate strategies to excel within it.

Chapter 8: Action Steps

1. Spend time with the chart in this chapter and assess your current operating position.
2. Give thought to the reality of your resources, opportunities and limitations, and determine if your current position is congruent with those resources.
3. Formulate strategies based upon the slot that best describes your market position.

Chapter 9

DISCOVERING: MORE PRODUCTIVE ADVERTISING

I'll be truthful, I have never really liked talking about advertising. Advertising is a dirty word to many storeowners, and who can blame them for thinking so? Advertising, after all, is something that's hard to wrap your head around.

Books and "experts" tell storeowners (though most of them know already) that advertising is a necessary element of managing a retail business, and budgets are written to allow for it. And yet, when it comes to a strategy for implementing that advertising, well, that is where advertising becomes even more of an enigma.

Perhaps the difficulty lies in monitoring the effectiveness of advertising, or perhaps it's just that the results are so darned intangible. Radio advertising, for example, occurs only through the transmission of invisible waves through the air. You can't hold sound waves in your hand, and often the only proof that radio advertising ever occurred is the bill you receive at the end of the month.

A newspaper or circular is not all that different. It's only ink on paper, and printed advertising's power to persuade is limited in time as well. I guess proponents of print might say, "Well, at least you can hold it in your hand." Yeah, you can, hooray!

Twenty years ago, as a sales representative for a hardware distributor, I enrolled almost all of my customers in the circular plan that our company offered. In the years that followed, it became increasingly difficult to convince customers that the circulars were a good thing. Circulars were simply not as effective as they had once been. I knew it and, obviously, the customers knew it, too.

But before we deal with how to increase the effectiveness of advertising, let's back up and address the fundamental question: Why do we advertise?

I have asked this question of dozens of retailers and received as many answers: to keep my name in front of the people; to draw *more* people into my store; to draw *new* people into my store; I don't know but you just have to do it; because everybody else does (my personal favorite); and many more.

Obviously, there seems to be a great deal of confusion about advertising. My hope is that, as you read through this chapter, you will gain a better understanding of why you advertise.

Every product and every service that was ever conceived by man for the purpose of selling, trading or bartering had to be marketed in some fashion. Before a product is purchased, it has to be wanted. Before a product is wanted, it has to have merit, which can take the form of need or the form of desire. For example, one obvious merit of food is that we need it to survive. Sure, we like the gourmet and treat foods too, but food is still a fundamental need. Conversely, a plasma television's merit lies in my desire as opposed to my need. Because I long for both the food and the television, the marketing of these two products catches my attention and jumpstarts my imagination.

Product marketers spend huge amounts of money to make their products the object of desire. Therefore, the products within your store produce a certain amount of pull on their own. The problem is that most of the products in your store are not unique to your store, but rather, they are available at a multitude of stores. So, it's important that you establish the uniqueness of your store, both in reality and in the imagination of your customers.

In short, just as the products are propelled by their brand name, your store has need for branding as well. And just as products themselves must be marketed, your store must be marketed, too. Because of this fact, store branding has become a popular topic of discussion in the hardware industry, and there have been a number of articles written on how best to accomplish this task.

First, a desire to patronize *your* store, *your* brand must be created. Memories must be encoded and habits must be formed. The supreme goal of your advertising, after all, is not that a consumer comes into your store one time, but that she becomes a regular customer.

Typically, we patronize the same places we have always patronized because such is our habit. These shops are encoded into our memories. Therefore, if we want to change peoples' shopping habits, we must first encode new memories into their minds. That is the purpose of advertising.

Experts tell us that there are two ways in which memories are encoded. This simple information can give you valuable insight into how you can best change people's behavior, how you can encourage them to think of *your* store first.

Here is a very important point: **Memories are encoded either by repetition or by emotional attachment.**

We have all heard that habits, both good and bad, are formed by repetition: When we default to our automatic guidance system or behavioural patterns, our encoded memories take over, manifesting as habits.

By way of example: we learned to tie our shoes through repetition. Someone showed us how and helped us repeat the process until, with diligent practice, the procedure became a memory, a skill and a habit. That memory is deeply engrained into our subconcious. We have repeated the procedure so many times, in fact, that we can tie our shoes with our eyes closed.

Contrast that form of memory encoding against a memory that is attached to a certain song — let's say the memory is a first kiss. When that song plays, you are instantly transported to that other time, that other place. Your memory of your first kiss is tied inextricably to that song, which acts as a delivery vehicle to bring the memory instantly to the forefront of your mind.

Unlike tying your shoes, your first kiss occurred only once, but that doesn't matter. The memory is still there. The difference is that the processes by which the two memories were encoded vary. One was encoded by repetition and the other through emotional attachment. The mechanism for encoding a memory doesn't matter either. Both memories are very real, and both are very accessible given the right stimuli.

You might say, "That's all well and good there, Seymour, but how does that guide me with my advertising? I don't think I can pass out that many first kisses."

Our first clue to successful advertising lies in the point of repetition. If you are going to advertise, work out a calendar that guides you through a repetitive process. Advertising people refer to this as "frequency," and although it may sound like "sales-speak" coming from a radio or newspaper representative, the fundamental truth underlying the recommendation is solid.

"But," you may be thinking, "I've got a budget. I can't continue to advertise if it's not doing me any good." This complaint is valid and invalid. If your advertising is doing no good, of course, it would be ludicrous to continue, but remember my contention that one of the most difficult aspects of advertising is measuring its effectiveness? Therein lies the problem.

Your store's goal is to show a profit, plain and simple. That is the single purpose of your store's existence. If the store does not profit, it will not continue to exist, and so the effectiveness of your advertising must be correlated with your profitability. The effectiveness of advertising can only be measured over time and against the benchmark of profitability.

Simply stated: Is your store's business increasing? Is profitability increasing? If the answers to these questions are yes, chances are good that your current advertising strategy is at least partially responsible for that improvement.

Remember the answers merchants gave me when I asked them why they advertised? *All* of those answers are right! All are valid reasons to advertise, but here's the problem: In order for advertising to effect the one true goal of your store, profitability, it must be part of a larger master plan.

If you are advertising sale-priced items at little or no margin, you must have a plan in place to offset the narrower margins that result from this pricing strategy. If the people who come in for your advertised merchandise buy nothing more, it is not the advertising that failed but the overall plan. People came to your store, but advertising can do more!

Did you display related items near the sale merchandise? Did your communication pieces tell your customers that they needed those related items to make their purchases complete? Were your employees fully educated on the merits of upselling? Did they know that suggestive selling is not an inconvenience to a customer, but rather, may save that customer an additional trip? Have you helped your clerks overcome their natural aversion to selling your customers more than they planned to buy?

Did your store's environment engage your customer at a level that later caused him to recall his shopping trip as a pleasant experience? Did he hear music that he enjoyed? Did he smell coffee or popcorn or some other aroma that helped elicit positive feelings? Did your use of color, displays, lighting and signage stimulate his senses and engage his imagination? Were there displays for him to touch and consider? Did he leave your store feeling good?

Obviously, advertising can not do the things I just mentioned, but nevertheless, if you want to build a fire under your advertising efforts, you must consider all of these elements, and ultimately they must all come together.

Forgive me if this is starting to sound a lot like my tirade on customer service. Indeed, we've considered these things before. The point that I want to emphasize is that all the elements of your store's operation are interconnected in such a fashion, with such synergy, that it takes microscopic examination to know where one ends and the next begins. Advertising is but one of those elements.

Your store's slot can also give you clues as to what might be the best strategy for your advertising efforts. For example, if you have determined that your store operates as a convenience store, then perhaps you should not advertise pricing.

I can hear your complaint now: "Advertising without pricing? That's like orange juice without sunshine, Hillary without Bill. Have you lost your mind?"

I have made the point previously, but it bears repeating. If your store operates as a convenience store, people do not frequent your store because of pricing. This is also true if your store operates within the product-driven niche slot. Your customers come to you for some reason other than pricing. If yours is a product-driven niche store, people come to you for your breadth of selection within a narrow category. If you are slotted as a convenience store, maybe it's your expertise, your location — or maybe you're the only game in town. The point is that, if your store is truly slotted as a convenience store or a product-driven niche store, then there are a number of reasons why advertising price may actually be counterproductive.

Consider these points: If your store is slotted as a convenience store, chances are good that your volume is moderate, at best. Another characteristic of a convenience store is a limited customer base. In short, because of these two important elements, it is of paramount importance that you maintain an above average margin in your store.

With this thought in mind, there are three counter-productive results that can occur when a convenience store advertises special prices. Let's say that you advertise an item with, what seems to you, a good price. Based upon your relative buying power, the margin is very slim — perhaps you're even selling the advertised item at cost. For the purpose of this discussion, let's say that your advertised item is in fact a loss leader (an old term that refers to selling something below cost to serve as a "come on" to prospective buyers).

You put your price out there only to discover that your competitors are advertising the same item at a price that is well below your price. Some would argue that there was simply not enough research on your part to determine what the advertised price should have been, but remember, in our scenario, you're already selling this product below cost.

Another knee-jerk reaction might be to blame your vendor, but remember, contrary to what some may tell you, size does matter. Your store's relatively low volume dictates your buying power.

Advertising pricing is an attempt to establish a pricing image. You have advertised a price, and immediately you have been trumped by your competitors. What image did this hypothetical set of events conjure in a prospective customer's mind? Worse yet, what message did it send to those people who are already your loyal customers? These "captive customers" have already established the habit of shopping at your store. Suddenly, right there in black and white, you've rubbed it in their face that they can buy this item for less somewhere else.

Perhaps your captive customer will go ahead and buy your advertised item, but here's another important point. Remember our buying equation from Chapter 3 If the Timeliness of Need coincides with the Timeliness of Availability, then a transaction will likely occur.

The obvious question then is: If he needed the item and he is truly your captive or regular customer, would he have purchased the item at your regular price anyway?

We have no way of knowing with any degree of certainty, of course, but the point is worth pondering. We definitely know that your margin has suffered. We also know that, if prospective customers are looking strictly at price, then you have lost the battle for their dollars because someone else had the item advertised at a lower price. Lastly in our counterproductive triumvirate, you actually paid — in advertising fees — for those lower margins and a negative price image!

It is important to remember that this logic does *not* apply to your store if it is slotted as a destination store, a regional competitor, or as a price-driven niche store. In each of these cases, you must advertise and establish your pricing prowess. Indeed, you must flex your muscle, play the game, and be prepared to be the "baddest-priced dude" in the valley.

One of the most important points in this whole discussion is that store managers must have a better feel for how the elements of the store's slot and advertising are interconnected. Accepting the characteristics that accompany your store's slot will give you a much more effective understanding of how to position your advertising.

The purpose of this discussion is not to tell a convenience store manager *not* to advertise, but only to suggest that a convenience store and a product-driven niche store should advertise something other than pricing.

As an aside, I have observed that one of the most effective means of advertising is to write educational or informational advertising articles. It is spring as I write this chapter, and many people's minds are turning to their lawns (I said many and I do not put myself in that group). These people are thinking about what they should do to ensure their grass pops up and their weeds fall down. Many of them don't know how to approach lawn care, and an article on this subject — one that outlines the proper chemicals, implements, and machinery to get lawn projects underway — would be well received. This type of advertising would have many advantages over one that relied on pricing to attract attention.

I'm going to take a small side trip here. Bear with me for a moment, and I believe you will eventually see the point that I want to make.

Working with dealers, I always found it fascinating that some circulars were real barn burners, while others failed miserably. Together, a storeowner and I would try to analyze the disparity in success rates between two ads by looking at the weather or by considering coinciding events, which certainly could have affected the results for the respective ads. However, there's something that probably had an even greater impact on the way those ads were received. It may sound over simplified, but here it is — the difference was simply item selection!

Remember our discussion earlier about the time of need equaling the time of availability and how those elements helped to consumate a transaction? If a circular advertising 40 items is distributed to 10,000 households, many of those circulars will immediately be trashed without ever being perused. Of the remaining households, and the people who actually look at the ads, only a fraction will have *need* for any of the 40 featured items. When they decide that their needs do not correlate with the circular's offering, they, too, will trash the ad. So you see, the effectiveness of the 10,000 distributed circulars inevitably will be diminished to some undeterminable degree. In short, the ad will do nothing to create need for its offering, so the success of the ad is at the mercy of this ratio of the community's existing desire.

Simply put, if June's results were indeed abysmal, nobody wanted what you offered in that month's ad.

Let's move back to our hypothetical informational ad on spring lawn care. Just like the pricing ad, the informational ad places your store's name in front of your audience. So score informational ad one and price-featured ad one.

However, an informational ad has the possibility of being clipped and saved for future reference and, therefore, often has a longer message life. I have not witnessed the same phenomenem with ads that featured price only.

In addition, where the pricing ad relies only on pre-existing desire or need, an informational ad can actually *create* desire and perceived need. The informational ad tells the story of how lawn care could be best accomplished, and the process just happens to require the things that you have available. Best of all, perhaps, by virtue of the article that you wrote on the subject, you are now perceived as an expert.

You have accomplished all of this without mentioning pricing, without sacrificing margin, and probably because of the typical abbreviated size of this type of ad, you have done all of these things with a smaller investment.

Now, let's move on to another point. Earlier in this chapter, I mentioned that there are two ways to encode memories. The first was repetition, and I think that we have dealt sufficiently with that topic. The experts tell us that the second way that memories are encoded is through emotional attachment. This is a key point and gives us additional clues into how we might make more efficient use of our promotional dollars.

Notice that I referred to promotional dollars, not advertising dollars. Advertising wears many disguises. Promotion of any kind is just another part of a total marketing effort. For example, if you offer your parking lot and other resources to a group of kids for their car wash, you have kept your store's name in front of this group of people. Because of your willingness to help the group, whether that group is affiliated with a school, church or other organization, you have underscored your support for that organization and their members.

This type of promotional effort spawns emotional attachment. It will not happen the first time that you undertake such an event. Once again, repetition factors into the ultimate success of the effort, but the important thing to remember is that the more involved you are in your community, the more the community will be involved with you.

A dealer lamented to me once that he had helped a particular group, but when it came time for the president of that group to make a large purchase, he seemed to have forgotten all about the help he had received and made his purchase elsewhere. What could I say? It's going to happen. There's no way to win them all, but once again, I would encourage you to be involved with as many groups as you can. You'll eventually win more than you'll lose, and the sum of your efforts will pay off even when microscopic slices don't.

Advertising? No, it's not fun to talk about, and it's hard to quantify advertising's results, but let's face it, if you're in business, you've got to play the game.

Chapter 9: Points to Remember

1. You must advertise for many reasons, including keeping your store's name in front of people, drawing more people into your store, drawing new people into your store, and because your competitors will be doing it.
2. Before products are purchased by consumers, they must be desired by consumers. This desire can be in the form of need or simple want.
3. Your advertising can help establish your store's branding. Your store's branding represents its unique qualities within the potpourri of choices that a consumer has in your trade territory.
4. You advertise to help consumers establish the habit of frequenting your store. Their habits are simply their encoded memories of experiences and their patterns of behaviour.
5. Memories can be encoded in one of two ways: frequency (repetition) or emotional attachment.
6. Frequency (repetition) is fundamental to establishing a successful advertising campaign.
7. Community involvment and attachment is key in addressing the emotional side of encoding shoppers' memories and patronage.
8. Advertising price is not the only way to advertise.
9. Advertising price may actually be counter-productive.
10. Slotting your store can help determine your best course of action for advertising.
11. In order to maximize your return on your advertising dollar, you must have all the elements of a positive shopping experience in place.

Chapter 9: Action Steps

1. Review Chapter 8 and reconfirm your store's slot within its trade community.
2. Analyze how your competitors are keeping their name in front of consumers.
3. Determine whether you want to meet your competitors head on or whether you would be best served by some other means of promotion.
4. Identify groups (civic organizations, clubs, schools, etc.) you would like to form a partnership with, and try to establish a relationship, seeking out mutually beneficial promotional ideas.
5. Assess upcoming seasonal changes and determine what informational ads you might write to appeal to large groups of people (i.e., gardening, lawn care, barbeque, gifts, decorating and painting techniques etc.).
6. Plan promotional events around your information advertisements. Perhaps bring in other experts for demonstrations and question-and-answer sessions.

DISCOVERING: YOUR COMPETITIVE POSITION

They're out there somewhere, trying to steal your customers and, all the while, keeping dibs on their own. They want more business! In fact, they want it all. They'll stop at nothing to fulfill their desire. They're studying and planning, setting goals and devising strategies, experimenting with décor and evolving nuances, all to change shoppers' habits and steal your customers! And if they can run you out of business along the way, well, "All's fair in love and war." Retail is certainly a war — a down and dirty in-the-trenches war for every available shopper's dollar.

That means you must be up to the challenge, that you must have a reconnaissance plan in place. You must know your competitors' businesses almost as well as you know your own. The better you know your competitors, the better you can position yourself within the marketplace; and the better you position yourself within the marketplace, the better the chance that your store will thrive in the midst of the war zone.

You must clearly understand your competition. If I were to ask you who your competitors are, you could more than likely list names, but simply knowing names is not enough. You must be intimately aware of the way your competitors position themselves in the marketplace. Are they, for example, driven by a pricing strategy or a selection strategy? How does your selection and pricing compare? Or do they hang their hats on customer service? If so, what do they offer that you don't?

Almost any astute observer would, at this juncture, point out that it is impossible to match selection and pricing with one of the big blue or orange stores, and that would be an accurate assessment. However, it is possible to become more closely matched by offering breadth in a category or two, becoming the top-level expert in those niches, and competing at a higher level. I have seen locations adopt this philosophy and survive quite well, thank you. They have discovered a product-driven niche style of operation.

The purpose of this monologue is not to persuade you to match anybody's selection or pricing, which would be ludicrous; but rather, to encourage you to become acutely aware of the differences between your operation and your competitors.

But it's not easy. Remember, when you analyze a competitor, you must do so through the eyes of a consumer. Ultimately, the consumer's opinion is the only one that matters. The consumer controls the dollars that both you and your competitors are striving to earn.

Objectively analyzing a competitor is a difficult process. The natural tendency is to make the assessment through your own, biased eyes. Your vision is obscured by the rose-colored glasses inevitably worn by someone who's already working long hours and doesn't want to hear that consumers desire even more hours of operation from your store. Without a system, it's difficult to take off those glasses and remove your perspective from the assessment.

The intention of this chapter is precisely to help you achieve a competitive assessment that is more informative and less biased. The plan is to give you a pre-scripted system that you can use "as is" or tweak to fit your needs.

We have designed a system to remove as much subjectivity from it as is possible. For example, if I asked two people to look at a group of stores and tell me which they considered the prettiest, I could conceivably get two different answers. The answers would be subject to the respondents' personal tastes, their judgment of the décor and overall aesthetics, and therefore, less revealing than a question constructed in an objective fashion. After all, beauty is in the eye of the beholder.

But if I asked those same two people which store was most recently built or remodeled, chances are they would give me the same answer. The answer to this question would not be subject to personal opinion, but rather, would be a simple matter of recalling the sequence of events.

Would the answer indicate which décor was the most pleasing or which environment was the most attractive? Of course not. But the dates of construction or the last remodel would indicate change within the respective stores. Those dates would represent movement and improvement. People are drawn to change and newness just as bugs are drawn to light. Even though this phenomenon is tempered by time, the dates of change indicate important data that we can reference, quantify, and then assign competitive values. Such values are the type of objective data that we are seeking because they give us unbiased feedback as to our store's position within the competitive arena, or to continue our analogy, within the war zone.

Here's another example of objectivity in the survey. We use figures from the Department of Transportation, which are often available on the Internet, to determine the number of cars that pass by each competitor's store. Location, after all, is critically important. Although these figures don't show ease of entry, they do show the relative exposure of the various locations.

Once we have determined traffic counts, we merely rank the stores in order. Our spreadsheet for analyzing your competitors is available at our website: www.discoverdbr.com. We call this tool the Competitive Assessment Barometer (C.A.B.). A screenshot of this valuable tool appears on the next page.

Objective Questions	Relative Value	Your Store DAVIDS	Store 2 ACE	Store 3 LOWES	Store 4 JBS FARM	Store 5
Rank all competitors in order of their showroom size.	100	2	3	1	4	
Rank all competitors according to total hours of operation.	80	3	1	2	4	
Rank all competitors by date of construction or last exterior remodel.	45	4	3	1	2	
Rank all competitors in order of D.O.T. traffic counts on frontage streets.	90	4	3	1	2	
Rank all competitors by date of last interior floor plan reset.	50	4	1	2	3	
Rank competitors according to the size of their parking lots.	70	4	2	1	3	
Rank competitors by the size of the largest exterior sign indentifying their building.	45	4	3	1	2	
Rank competitors by the highest levels of interior lighting.	35	2	1	2	3	
Rank competitors by the amount of retail shopping within a 3 block area.	100	4	3	1	4	
Give those competitors with parking lot pylon signs a 1...those without a 4.	60		1	1	1	

Step 1. Fill in the names of the stores in the bright green squares. Your store is listed first.

Step 2. Rank from 1-5 the position of the stores in regard to the question. If you feel that two stores rank equally give them the same ranking. Notice the instructions on questions in lines 13 and 31.

Step 3. Press the "Print Report" Button in the center of the screen.

Print Report

Subjective Questions	Relative Value	DAVIDS	ACE	LOWES	JBS FARM
Rank all competitors in the order of your perception of the cleanliness of their store.	55				
Rank all competitors as to the ease of entering their parking area.	45				
Rank competitors by the number of exposures to their advertising in a week.	75				
Rank competitors by your perception of the expertise of their clerks.	60				
Rank competitors by your perception of the time required to consumate a purchase.	45				
Rank competitors by your perception of their merchandising or presentation.	65				
Rank competitors by their active involvement in the community.	85				
Rank competitors as to your perception of the general repair of their building.	45				
Rank competitors as to your perception of the pleasantness of the smell of the store.	30				
Rank all competitors with background music as 1...those without as 4.	25				

The spreadsheet is quite colorful (although it appears in grayscale in this book) and appears complex. Although the spreadsheet is designed to process many equations, the user's interface is actually quite simple and straightforward. The instructions are written in the gray area. Once you have filled out the information, you simply press the "Print Report" button and the spreadsheet generates a seven-page report that will give you valuable insight into your competitive position.

As I mentioned earlier, we designed the C.A.B. to function quite well as is, but you can modify it, if you like. During its creation, we interviewed a number of store managers, others involved in retail businesses and consumers. We asked them which characteristics of a store's operation were the most important to consumers.

Then, based upon those answers, we assigned relative values to our assessment questions. The cells labeled "relative value" indicate the values we attached to the spreadsheet questions.

You can modify these numbers if you like, but at least one of the cells should be assigned a value of 100, and all other questions must be rated relative to that cell(s). If you feel that two questions are of equal value and that they are the most important considerations, you should assign both a value of 100, as you see in the sample questionnaire. If another question is only half as important as the quality assigned 100, you would assign it a value of 50. When you open the spreadsheet, you will see the values other experts and consumers suggested that we assign to the various questions. Remember, you should always use the same values the next time you do the survey. In this way, you can benchmark your store's relative position within its changing competitive arena over time.

As stated earlier, we felt it extremely important to remove as much subjectivity from the process as possible. For example, our panel of experts and consumers felt that breadth of selection was the number one consideration in a consumer's decision-making process. Because even this question seemed somewhat subjective (e.g., you might rate a selection better than I would), we changed the question to read, "Rank the competitors by the square-footage size of their showroom."

The size of a showroom will typically (although, we concede, not always) reflect its breadth of selection. The size of a showroom, however, is not at all subjective. This store has the biggest showroom, this store the next biggest, and so. We can easily assign ranks to this objective indicator.

You are probably wondering (I would be), "But what about price? Isn't that the number one consideration in consumers' minds?"

Price is very important, but with this particular assessment, we are focusing on *environmental* and *operational* attributes. We are **concentrating on the shopping experience.**

Price should never be overlooked, of course, but to draw conclusions about pricing from small samples can be counterproductive and potentially misleading. Therefore, competitive price shops should be repeated regularly with assorted merchandise before drawing any conclusions about your store's price position within the marketplace.

I have repeated the mantra that you must keep your study objective; however, you will notice in the C.A.B. screenshots, as well as in the spreadsheet itself, if you choose to download it, that we had to leave some subjective questions in the mix. There was just no way around it.

The spreadsheet consists of ten questions that are structured quite objectively and ten that leave more to interpretation. Therefore, whoever starts the process should finish the process. With the same person doing the evaluation, the outcome should be consistent. In fact, it would be interesting to have two individuals complete the entire process to determine what differences, if any, the two studies would produce.

The process itself should not take a lot of time. You will know the answers to some of the questions immediately. Others will require a walk-through of your competitors' stores, but that is something that you should do regularly anyway. The walk-through need not be long and grueling. In fact, you should be able to gather most of the information required for the C.A.B. in minutes.

Once you have the information, simply rank the competitors (your store included) within each question. As an example, you will see that the first of the objective questions requires that you rank all of the test stores by showroom size. The biggest would receive the number one ranking; the smallest the number five ranking. Please note that the spreadsheet is set up for a maximum of five stores. You can test fewer if you choose, however — the spreadsheet will make the appropriate calculations.

After you have completed the questionnaire, activate the process and print button, and the application will print a report that ranks your store's overall score, along with scores for a number of sub-groupings that you should find interesting.

The point of the exercise is not the final score (although you should work to improve the number). The purpose of the procedure is to sensitize you to the many things that are affecting your store's performance. As you become more aware of the mental processes that a consumer engages in to determine where he shops, some consciously, some unconsciously, you will be better equipped to modify your store to appeal to more people.

Let's take a look at an actual report that the spreadsheet generated.

Competitive Assessment Barometer (C.A.B.) Report

Thanks for using the Competitive Assessment Barometer. We think that you will find it to be a valuable tool in your quest for store improvement. Constant improvement, as you know, is a must. Your store is dynamic and your marketplace ever-changing. It is important that you keep abreast of these changes and align your store to take advantage of this constantly changing environment. This study can help you do that.

Hereafter, we will refer to the Competitive Assessment Barometer as C.A.B. The C.A.B. uses mathematical equations to give you a great deal of feedback from the 20 questions that you ranked your store against your competitors' stores. You should complete this process annually in order to chart your store's progress over time.

If you did not override the suggested values assigned to the spreadsheet, you will notice that the highest values are given to showroom size, frontage traffic counts, and retail pull in the area. Two of these values are specific to location, and the old realtors' mantra of "location, location, location" is rewarded both at this level of the spreadsheet as well as within the internal equations. The rationale, of course, is that more is better when it comes to exposure.

This report contains information sorted and evaluated from a number of perspectives. It can be confusing, but we want you to gain as much from it as you can.

Your study consisted of four stores including your own. Store 2 ranked as the top-performing store in your trade territory with a rough score of 13,830. Your store ranked third of the four competitors with a rough score of 6,395. The rough score refers to the total composite values assigned to both the objective and subjective portions of the assessment questionnaire.

You will see two charts on the following page. The first chart represents the rough scores of all of the competitors in your study. The second chart takes those rough scores and regenerates them into a more easily analyzed percentile format. This chart computes the sum of the assessed points as a fraction of the whole. Don't misunderstand this as representing the total of the available business, for in many cases, the two top-performing retailers dominate the marketplace.

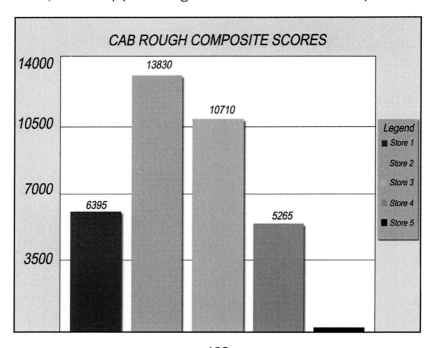

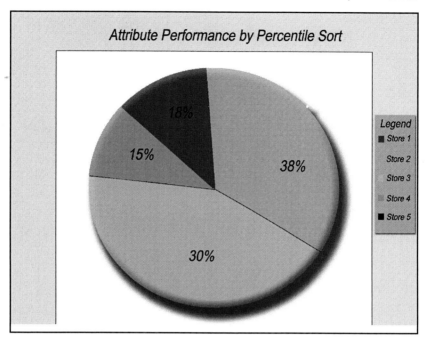

This chart illustrates that, of all points dispensed, Store 2 received 38 percent of those total points. As illustrated, the chart distributes the balance of the points.

The next chart illustrates the breakdown for points assigned to the **objective** half of the assessment questionnaire, which contained the most valuable store qualities. Two of these high-value attributes, frontage highway counts and retail pull within a three-block radius, are not within your control unless relocation is possible. However, historical data and expert opinion support the importance of these somewhat static qualities. We elected to use raw data points to let you know where your store stood in this very important contrast.

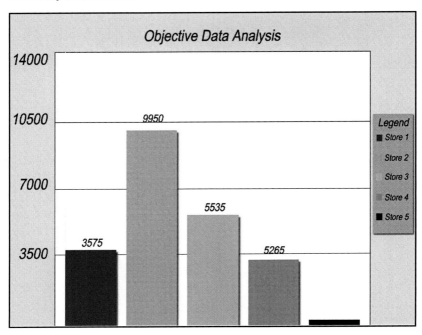

If your store is number one or two in this portion of the assessment, the objective criteria in the study are not hindering your store's performance. If your competitors dominate your store in this portion of the assessment, however, and you are trying to operate as a destination store or regional competitor, your best strategy probably lies in reexamining your store's slot. Perhaps you should consider transforming your store into a product-driven niche store, for example (See Chapter 8 of Discovery Based Retail). A product-driven or price-driven niche store is not as affected by location, traffic pull, or building size as is a destination store or a regional competitor slotted store.

It is also worth mentioning that the stores with which you compare your store should be your head-to-head competitors and not those that merely overlap in a few areas.

This is especially true if you are already operating as a niche store. Unless your competitor shares the same niche, and product and services offering, it may be difficult to make a head-to-head comparison.

The following subjective point totals represent elements that are readily within your control. This is not as true with the characteristics isolated in the objective sections, where many of the considerations are site specific.

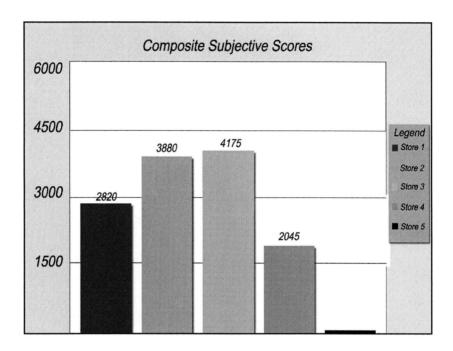

Your store **should** have the highest marks in this portion of the analysis. Remember, other than the question about ease of entry into your parking area, you can control every other attribute of the subjective analysis. For many of these items, you can start implementing plans to change today. Participating in this exercise is simply a waste of time unless you act upon what you have learned. Call your team together today, share this data with them, and start planning your strategy!

Let's take a look at some other information the C.A.B reveals. You probably noticed that the questions in the survey were color-coded. The aqua sections pertain to the environmental characteristics of the shopping experience in your store and in your competitors' stores. The following chart illustrates how your store performed in this important comparison. This chart will give you a "feel" for the way consumers might contrast the shopping experience in the various stores.

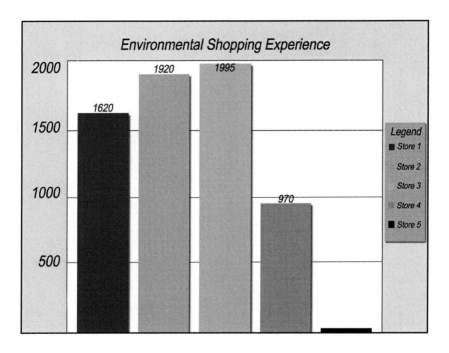

How effectively do you and your competitors communicate with consumers? As we discussed in Discovery Based Retail, effective advertising is based on repetition, or ad frequency, and emotional attachment, i.e. sponsoring community events to create customer loyalty. We structured the questions highlighted in orange on the C.A.B. to determine the type of repetition and community involvement that will foster success.

The spreadsheet's inner-workings put a premium on both frequency of advertising and involvement of store personnel within the community. In his book The Paradox of Choice, Barry Schwartz makes a good case for what he calls "opportunity costs." (12) His point is that any choice about anything includes "costs." To apply his premise to a most elemental example, if I go out to dinner tonight and order chicken,

I not only have the cost of the chicken but I have the cost of not being able to order the beef or fish. Those are "opportunity costs."

Here's how this concept of cost applies to your "community involvement. Let's say that you are active in and/or supportive of a particular civic group or organization in your community. If another member of that group makes purchases elsewhere, each time that he greets you he must "pay the opportunity costs" of having to acknowledge, even if only to himself, that he did not support someone who supported his group. This is a powerful motivation. Consequently, community involvement for a store manager and her personnel are important everywhere, but they are **critical** *in small towns. Remember this falls within advertising as promotion.*

The following chart shows the results of that part of the questionnaire.

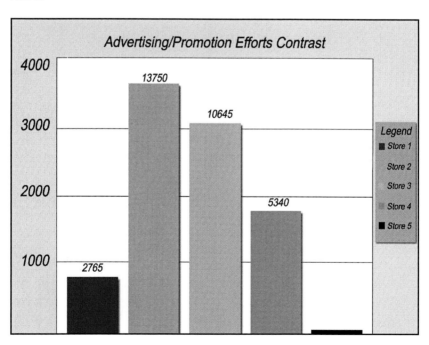

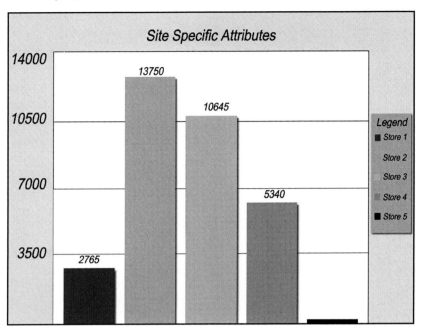

The final chart contrasts site-specific attributes. We highlighted the questions that we used for this contrast in bright pink. Typically, relocation is the only way to change these characteristics. If you are considering that, you can actually use the C.A.B. to help you weigh your options. Once again, if your site is prohibiting you from reaching your goals, you should consider how it is influencing your business. If your store receives low marks on this section of the C.A.B. and relocation is absolutely not an option, we encourage you to review your store's slot and reevaluate your strategy. See Chapter 8 of Discovery Based Retail.

End of Report

We want to emphasize that the numbers are not as important as the process. However, the numbers give you an easy way to quantify the data that you accumulate. If you have questions *about the spreadsheet, or if you have suggestions for its improvement, please email us at administrator@discoverdbr.com.*

Obviously, you could go through a similar process with a piece of paper and a pencil. You could mark which of your competitors does what the best, but unfortunately, there would be little that you could do with the information you gather.

The C.A.B. gives you not only a way to evaluate where you stand within your trade territory today, but also a benchmark with which to monitor your store's progress over time.

Chapter 10: Points to Remember

1. Your competitors will know your operation; you need to learn about theirs.
2. The better you know your competitors, the better you can align the tactical position of your store within the war zone.
3. Your competitive analysis needs to be as objective as possible, as if viewed through a consumer's eyes.
4. The person who begins the assessment process should finish it. In this manner, the data will remain the most consistent.
5. The spreadsheet that our company uses is available for download at www.discoverdbr.com.

Chapter 10: Action Steps

1. Either download the spreadsheet that we use or formulate one of your own. Compose it in a fashion that will weigh the different characteristics of each store that you are examining from a consumer's perspective.
2. Divide your analysis into two sections, the questions you can pose objectively and those you cannot.
3. Give the highest assessment points to the site attributes that are intrinsic to your location. These attributes are typically not subject to change, but what you discover about them will give you an "eyes open" perspective on your store's situation.
4. Assign a key member or two from your staff to complete the exercise or complete it yourself. Make it clear to the surveyors that their task is not to make your store "look good," but rather, to provide an honest and accurate assessment of your store's current situation.
5. If you have two people complete the reports, examine their results and check for glaring differences, as well as for data that has the most impact. After reviewing this data with key personnel, schedule a store meeting and discuss your plans for improving your store's C.A.B. Score.

If you have questions regarding the report, or if you have suggestions to make it even more powerful, please email us at admininstrator@discoverdbr.com.

DISCOVERING: BETTER SALES FLOOR PRODUCTIVITY (Hitting on all Cylinders)

The metaphor above is not new, but an oft-used reference to an automobile engine's state of performance. If, for example, an 8-cylinder engine has a fouled plug or two, it is "not hitting on all cylinders." It may run and, in fact, it probably will, but it will not produce the same amount of power as it would if it were properly tuned and all of the cylinders were contributing to the performance of the whole. The engine's idle would be rough, and power and acceleration would be greatly diminished. Even the new computer-controlled engines, which operate on only a portion of their cylinders under certain conditions, are the most powerful when all of their cylinders are firing.

Perhaps, as my metaphor suggests, it's time to take a look at your showroom's sales performance and assess its need for a tune-up. Is your sales engine firing on all cylinders? Or simply put, does your sales space produce at its maximum potential?

Within your showroom, a number of different departments are allotted sales space. You have to heat these spaces, light these spaces, and staff these spaces. Doesn't it make sense, then, to periodically contrast department against department and discover clues as to how the space could be more productively utlized and more profitably aligned?

In a perfect store in a perfect world, each square foot of your store's sales space would perform at an equal and optimum level and well above the industry standards. Ours, however, is not a perfect world, and few of you are in charge of perfect stores.

That means we have to make the best of what we've got, and that's what this chapter is about. In earlier chapters, we discussed getting people to move through every zone of your store. We discussed attributes that make shoppers more likely to linger longer and buy more while they're there. But even with all of those bases covered and those opportunities addressed, your store will still have deviations in departmental performance. We will never change that completely, but just as you would do with an engine periodically, there are maintenance steps that you can take to improve your store's showroom sales performance.

Let's start with a most fundamental and elementary premise. *You should be working to increase and balance your store's sales per square foot.* Please, though, before you respond with "well...duh," contemplate just how you would go about trying to increase **sales per square foot** in just **one** department if it were performing at a level far lower than your other departments.

Of course, most of us would consider ways to create more *total sales* in that given department. If we successfully increased that department's sales, and provided that the footprint of the department did not increase, then we would have acheived our goal.

There is another way though. If we took that same department and streamlined the offering, or in some other way condensed the amount of space that the department occupied, we would thereby shrink the department's footprint. Then, provided we were still able to produce the same amount of total sales, we would have had the same effect. We would have, just as in the earlier example, increased our department's sales per square foot. This is true simply because we produced the same amount of sales in a smaller area. It's a matter of simple division.

You might ask, however, "Did we increase sales or profitability?" And the answer, of course, would be no. We simply reallocated floor space, but condensing that one department would facilitate the luxury of expanding departments that are producing at higher levels or to bring in new categories. Think of this first move as being something like the individual moves in solving those the little puzzles, where you slide pieces back and forth and up and down, thereby allowing movement of the other pieces, until finally, if you are persistent, the picture can be completed.

After having reset many stores in my career, I can say confidently that there are *always* ways to condense the space that a department occupies. Sometimes its as simple as merchandising a gondola tighter by moving products closer together. Other times it involves having two facings of some items instead of four, or using longer pegboard hooks. Still other times it means combing through the department to look for dogs or dead items, taking them out of your layout, cutting your losses and moving on (something that should be done on a regular basis anyway). Gondolas can be raised and aisle widths narrowed slightly. The important point here is to start thinking of ways to facilitate improvement. Consider shrinking and expanding departments, calculating what effect those maneuvers would have on your store's total profitability.

A critical point in this mental process, of course, is determining how the departments are contributing to the whole of your store's sales when contrasted against each other. It's impossible to recognize your best producing department without knowing the relationship of both the sales per square foot and the inventory dollars per square foot. Is your highest sales-dollar producing department your best department? Not necessarily.

How much space and how many inventory dollars does it take to "fire that particular cylinder"? What are the "opportunity costs" of making that department your highest sales producer? In other words, what is sacrificed in the other departments to make those sales possible? Does the size of the highest dollar producing department dominate the sales floor? If so, are you driving the total dollars sales volume of that department simply by its larger presentation, and if that's the case, what did you have to condense and sacrifice to make that possible?

Or does the department produce the higher sales results while working with only a small portion of your total showroom? If that is the case, then what would be possible with a more extensive presentation of this department's wares?

Here's the problem: The space of each department is interrelated with the space that the other departments occupy. Unless you add space to your store through expansion, the sales space, obviously, does not grow. Your store has the same amount of square feet today that it did last week. So, if a department grows, space must be taken from another department, while a shrinking department leaves space that must be reallotted. Unfortunately, the complications don't stop there, either.

There's the small matter of inventory. Your inventory is currently budgeted in relationship to your sales. Once again, in an ideal world, your store's inventory would be equitably balanced across the whole of the showroom. It never is, of course, because of simple facts, like it's a whole lot easier to get inventory dollars per square foot tied up in power tools or accessories than it is in PVC fittings. Nonetheless, we should still use the departmental inventory/dollar balance to guide our managerial decisions regarding category realignments. We should strive for optimization!

As an aside, there's also the matter of the differing margins produced by different departments. Those margins, of course, are critical in assessing the *profitablity* of each respective department. For this study, however, we are considering two elements only: sales per square foot and the inventory dollars per square foot that are required to drive those sales. This is a delicate balance, and one on which many retailers fail to focus.

We talked about the space of each department being interconnected, or somewhat "rubber-banded" together. We could say that the same theory is in play with the total inventory dollars that you have at your command. Although budgets are not as physical or as solid as your store's walls, your inventory budgets have limitations that are just as real, just as tangible. In this case, however, the limitation is the amount of total funds available. Therefore, if we expand the inventory of one department, it makes sense to consider the other departments' inventories and decide which one we might reduce to "free up" the funds required for the planned expansion.

But now we've further complicated the situation because we have two sets of rubber-banded equations that we are trying to balance simultaneously: floor space and inventory. As if that weren't enough, these two equations are also inextricably tied to each other.

Take a look at our Space and Inventory Enhancement Calculator on the following page. The chart shows information entered for a hypothetical 5100-square-foot hardware store. The first column indicates the department names. The second column is the total square feet devoted to that department.

The total square feet selected for this type of examination should always reconcile with the total square feet of your store. To calculate your departmental size, measure halfway into the aisles of the adjacent departments. This space facilitates the display, and *the space in the aisles must be accounted for* and "charged" to a department. You will notice that the chart also shows the space devoted to service areas. This area must also be recognized and reconciled because service areas obviously take up usable space within your store.

				Space Productivity Ratio		Inventory Holding Ratio	
Department	Sq. Feet	Inventory	Sales	Sales Per Ft.	SPR	Inventory Per Ft.	IHR
Plumbing	800	$ 38,000	$ 84,750	$ 106	103.15%	48	114.96%
Electrical	500	$ 35,000	$ 63,000	$ 126	122.69%	70	169.42%
Hardware	1200	$ 40,200	$125,124	$ 104	101.53%	34	81.08%
Lawn and Garden	900	$ 37,000	$138,000	$ 153	149.30%	41	99.50%
Hand Tools	500	$ 23,225	$ 47,500	$ 95	92.50%	46	112.42%
Power Tools	800	$ 35,000	$ 58,000	$ 73	70.59%	44	105.88%
Service Areas	400	$ 2,300	$ 7,400				
Sub Totals	5100	$ 210,725	$ 523,774				

	Total Feet	Ttl Inventory	Ttl. Sales	Ttl Sales per Ft	Ttl. Inventory Per Ft.	Turns
Totals	5100	$ 210,725	$ 523,774	$ 103	$ 41.32	2.49

RESET

The bottom row cell, labeled "Ttl Sales Per Ft.," indicates that our imaginary store produced total sales of $103 per square foot. By looking at the individual departments in the same column, you can see how each one compared.

The letters SPR label one column, which is an acronym for the Space Productivity Raio. This column translates the sales per square foot figures into percentile ratios. The average of $103 per square foot sales becomes 100 percent, and then all of the other departments are contrasted against this "norm" or "standard." For example, the plumbing department produced at a little over 103% of the store's average rate per square foot, with sales of $106 per foot.

This spreadsheet guides you through a very enlightening process. It gives visual clues about problem areas in your store and also highlights areas of "hidden" opportunities. You will see that the power tool department's Space Productivity Ratio is shaded in red. The red cell indicates that the department produced at an anemic rate of 70.59% of the average. The logical fix for a department that produces relatively low dollars per square foot is to decrease the department size, isn't it? But by how much? And what do you do with the space that you've freed up? But wait, it's even more complicated!

Remember that all of the departments are rubber-banded together. If you shrink one department and expand another, every ratio will change because no department operates autonomously. The goal is to balance the productivity of your showroom floor, but remember that you have to do so while maintaining a balance of inventory, as well.

Now, let's switch gears for a second. Notice that there are two cells in the Space Productivity Ratio column that are highlighted in yellow. The spreadsheet highlights these cells automatically, providing a visual clue that there may be hidden opportunities in these departments. Since the electrical and lawn and garden departments are producing at much higher relative rates per square foot, it's logical to assume that more space in these areas might translate to even greater sales.

So, using the process described above to shrink one department to facilitate the expansion of another, let's examine the results of just two such maneuvers. We will decrease the size of the Power Tool department and increase the Lawn and Garden area, both by 300 square feet. The following screenshot shows the results of those two changes.

We no longer have any red areas in the Space Productivitiy Ratio column, which is obviously a positive change. Unfortunately, however, we have another inventory cell that has turned red. The red cell in the power tool inventory column indicates that, if we decrease the size of the sales area devoted to power tools to 500 square feet, we are also going to have to make an inventory adjustment.

The next screenshot has the two changes keyed in for adjusting the department size of the power tool and lawn and garden sections.

Department	Sq. Feet	Inventory	Sales	Sales Per Ft.	SPR	Inventory Per Ft.	IHR
Plumbing	800	$ 38,000	$ 84,750	106	103.15%	$ 48	114.96%
Electrical	500	$ 35,000	$ 63,000	126	122.69%	$ 70	169.42%
Hardware	1200	$ 40,200	$ 125,124	104	101.53%	$ 34	81.08%
Lawn and Garden	1200	$ 37,000	$ 138,000	115	111.98%	$ 31	74.62%
Hand Tools	500	$ 23,225	$ 47,500	95	92.50%	$ 46	112.42%
Power Tools	500	$ 35,000	$ 58,000	116	112.95%	$ 70	169.42%
Service Areas	400	$ 2,300	$ 7,400				
Sub Totals	5100	$ 210,725	$ 523,774				

Total Feet	Ttl Inventory	Ttl Sales	Ttl Sales per Ft		Ttl. Inventory Per Ft.	Turns
5100	$ 210,725	$ 523,774	$ 103	$0	$ 41.32	2.49
Store Total Feet 5100	$ -					
0						

RESET

155

After you have experimented with various departmental changes and have finished the analytical process, the aqua cells will alert you to the changes that you'll need to schedule to start manifesting the tune-up of your store.

Refer back to the screenshots of the spreadsheet now. Notice that only the inventory ratio of the electrical department was highlighted in red. This department held 169% of the average inventory of our store's total sales space.

After we changed the department sizes of the power tool and the lawn and garden areas, however, the inventory cell for power tools turned red, as well. This signifies that, if we make our proposed changes, the inventory in the power tool section would also be extreme in relationship to our store's average inventory per square foot.

At this point in the process, we would experiment with various fixes for the new problem. We could lower the inventory of the power tool department or we could lower the proposed department expansion to under 300 feet. For example, with only a 200-foot expansion, the power tool inventory holding ratio cell might turn green again.

Of course, if you lowered the inventory in the power tool department, that would free up funds for increasing the inventory in one of the better performing departments, but then the other departmental ratios would change, too. Remember everything is rubber-banded together.

Hopefully, by now you have a feel for how this tweaking process works. It is a management method that employs action instead of reaction. You become the mechanic that tunes the engine of your store's operation, and your store will perform better when inventory and sales per square foot are optimally balanced for their highest productivity.

It's worth mentioning here that the results of the spreadsheet are driven entirely from the data that you input. Although the sales represented in this example are far below national averages for hardware stores as reported by the NRHA, for the purpose of this exercise, it doesn't matter; no national averages or indexes are inherent in the inner-workings of the spreadsheet. *It examines the ratios in your store only.* Therefore, this data can guide you through changes for improving your store at whatever level your store is currently producing.

Also, you can collect the same data without using our spreadsheet. It is simply a matter of running the various equations. However, the exact process that I have described in this chapter would be difficult without our spreadsheet or one like it to help you analyze the changes that you are exploring. We established the acceptable ranges, and this is the tool that we use in our consulting work.

That said, if for some reason you do not undertake the process in *exactly* this fashion, that's fine too. However, I challenge you to take an active managerial approach to evaluating your various departments, their sales and their inventories, and how they are intrinsically linked to one another. One final thought: Although our background is in the hardware industry, this process is applicable to any retail store, any product offering.

Chapter 11: Points to Remember

1. Each department of your store requires a percentage of your showroom's available floor space. It is important to determine how each department contributes to sales in relationship to that space allotment.
2. Every department also "holds inventory." It is important to assess how the inventory holding ratio of each department contributes to the whole of your store's performance.
3. Because both the space productivity ratio and the inventory holding ratio refer to numbers that are portions of a whole, each equation is rubberbanded. In other words, a change in one department will produce changes in all of the departments.
4. Because of these rubberbanded equations, there are "opportunity costs" that accompany every decision. For example, if I expand my plumbing area, I pay the cost of having to shrink another department. Likewise, if I devote more of my inventory dollars to lawn and garden, I must "free-up" those dollars from another department or increase my overall inventory budget. In short, both space and inventory budgets are limited, and therefore, I must decide where to allot each valuable resource.
5. When completing this managerial exercise, you must reconcile **all** of the sales floor space. The service areas and aisles must be "charged" to the various departments.
6. There are two ways to increase departmental sales per square foot. You can: (A.) Increase the department's sales while maintaining a consistent amount of floor space devoted to the department, or (B.) you can maintain current sales within the department while reducing the footprint that the department occupies.
7. Extreme variations in Sales Productivity Ratios and/or Inventory Holding Ratios spotlight both trouble areas and areas of opportunity.

Chapter 11: Action Steps

1. Go to our website page called productivity at www.discoverdbr.com and watch the video tutorial on the Space and Inventory Enhancement Calculator. Download our calculator to use for your discovery process or create your own spreadsheet.
2. Make plans to complete this exercise with your key personnel. Use a floor plan drawing of your store's current layout and assess where to define its deparmental boundaries. Measure halfway into the adjacent aisles to fully account for all of the space. Decide how you will "charge" the space for the customer service areas. One good way is to distribute that space amongst the various departments in relationship to the total space that the department occupies. When you are done, you should be able to reconcile the number of feet in your study with the square footage of your showroom.
3. If you use our Space and Inventory Enhancement Calculator, the aqua cells will alert you to the changes you need to make. Once you have processed this information and have developed a clear understanding of the positive changes that you can make, develop a timeline for implementing those changes. For example, you may develop a 4-month plan to reduce the inventory in one department in order to "free-up" funds and expand another. But remember, the key is to keep your eye on the end result. If you know where you must go, you can make plans to get there!

Chapter 12

DISCOVERING: SAFE-HARBOR BALANCED PRICING

I know, "Safe-Harbor Balance" is a strange title for a chapter name in a book about retailing. I considered several other titles, but I kept coming back to this one. I liked the imagery that the title suggests — ships anchored securely in calm waters.

"Yeah, that's all well and good," you might say, "but what does it have to do with pricing in a retail store?"

Waves of information, theories, and methodologies crash back and forth creating turbulence and uncertainty for retailers. Navigation through these choppy waters is best left to seasoned captains. However, even the most seasoned captain should consider all of the routes available to him. Ultimately you want the ship that is your store, to be anchored securely in the calm waters of profitability.

Safe harbor balanced pricing is pricing that the majority of your customers perceive as acceptable but is also sufficient to produce a fair and reasonable profit given the investment in your store.

To achieve balanced pricing may take some adjustments on your part, but don't dismiss the importance of this tweaking process. I recall working with a hardware dealer in a rural community not many years ago who was still using the keystone method of pricing. He had learned the hardware business from his father, and keystoning had served them well for years. His frustration rested in the fact that, although he would often sell plumbing accessories, he seldom sold water heaters or closet combinations, both of which, of course, are the project starters. Mike decided to undertake a change to his retail-pricing methodology, and I guided him through it.

In a subsequent store visit, he was all smiles and told me that he had sold more water heaters in the eight weeks since the changes than he had sold in the previous ten years. That figure might be sufficiently impressive, but what was most notable is how Mike's business began to climb to a new level. He shifted from a defeatist attitude to one of being able to compete. It was gratifying to watch the fire ignite in him and spread to his staff. Within a year, Mike and his employees remodeled the store and quite literally reinvented themselves.

Mike was like the coon dog in an old story. The dog was in excruciating pain from sitting on its own tail. He sat there howling, not knowing that he need only move and the pain would go away. Likewise, once Mike began moving forward, his problems began to mysteriously disappear, too. He began to see opportunities that had previously eluded him

Setting new retails, however is a tricky undertaking. It requires the ability to predict with some certainty how the prices will be perceived by your customers, but that's not the only challenge. Some type of dynamic forecasting relevant to the end product of price changes as regards profitability is also necessary. In other words, the system should have forecasting abilities based upon historic purchases. Of course, some modern point-of-sale systems help with this function if utilized to their full potential, but these systems do not have the broad base of industry price information nor the local research that facilitates sound decisions. Therefore, your supplier seems the logical place to start implementing a variable hardware pricing structure, but remember, their recommendations are only starting points. As an aside, remember my hardware background and change hardware to whatever products you are selling.

When I warn not to let your vendor's "starting point" recommendations for retail pricing lull you into complacency, please don't misinterpret my message.

There's not an evil conspiracy on the part of vendors to purposely position your store with the wrong retail prices. That wouldn't make sense. Your vendors try to insure that your store stays competitive, which is of course in their best interest.

Philip H. Mitchell

Just remember that your vendors are working within the limitation of their "big picture" view of the industry. Hopefully, they've done their homework and they know the prevalent prices of the items that they provide. They are, no doubt, painfully aware that all of their customers operate in an ultra-competitive environment.

But are your vendors factoring in the competitive slot of your store? Do they know how your store fits into its *specific* community? Do they know the amount of profit that your store must generate to stay viable and produce the fair and reasonable return that I mentioned? Are they using pricing from major-market destination stores to form their recommendations for your convenience or product-driven niche slotted store? *Ultimately, your store's profitability is your responsibility, not your vendors'.*

Back when I was Vice President of Sales for a hardware wholesaler, and had the responsibility of training salespeople to work with store managers on establishing their retail prices, I instructed them to tell their customers that our "system" would paint their pricing with broad brushstrokes.

I told salespeople to keep this analogy in mind and to tell their customers that broad brushstrokes do not complete a work of art. A masterpiece can only be created by paying attention to details and subtle nuances, and if those retailers wanted to create a pricing system that was truly a "work of art," they would have to finish their own painting.

The distributor that I worked for has one of the best retail price guidance systems available. I say that confidently because we actually shopped prices at our customers' local competitors' stores. Checking pricing at a local level is of paramount importance — this was not a one-size-fits-all system of pricing! But even as good as that company's system was, it was not comprehensive. That is the point that I'm trying to convey.

The local price shop that was done for our retailers was a one-time occurence, or perhaps, at best, a biennial event for those dealers who understood the benefits. Using those small samples of price shops, we extrapolated data and made blanket changes across a wide spectrum of products. When considering what is available at the vendor level, this is as good as it gets.

Our customers, who had witnessed increased profit margins because of the price shops and the subsequent price adjustments, would eventually consider repeating the process.

Now, allow me to switch gears and tell you about an interaction that I had recenly with a client of DBR. Our company performs comprehensive store assessements, seeking out new avenues of profitability. We sometimes present what we discover in a DVD format. This unique method of presentation allows our customers to evaluate and digest the information at their leisure, and they can revisit the information as many times as they wish after our initial meeting.

Recently, after one such presentation, our client, the store manager, took exception to the section that we had completed on his retail pricing. He defended his supplier, saying that many of the items on the price-check portion of the presentation were on his vendor's top 100 list. He said that his vendor felt that it was important that he be priced competitively on those items — and he certainly was — but here was the problem: Of the 30 items that we price-shopped, his store priced 27 of those items lower than his primary local competitor, a destination store. His store is a product-driven niche store that does a nice business, but primarily in a very narrow category. His store struggles with profitability and constantly fights to maintain adequate margins to fuel improved performance.

The margin that he was giving away on these key items was doing nothing to attract additional business! The other elements that would have made him a player in the categories we price shopped were not addressed. The destination store he competed against was huge, and although his store was moderate in size, it was still much smaller. The destination store was positioned at a location that had higher frontage road traffic, and therefore, was more visible. The competitor's store was in a location of higher retail-traffic pull as well. You get the picture. His decision to operate as a product-driven niche store, given these facts was right on.

His customers were not coming to him because of his store's pricing on these key items, and even with lower retails, he could not "buy business" away from the destination store. So, in the final analysis, all the lower pricing on these key items did was lower his store's margin.

The vendor's pricing design was not flawed. It simply was not aligned with the pricing model of a product-driven niche store. The price-shopped items that he was selling were simply being picked up as a convenience by the captive shoppers partaking of his niche business offering.

So should he competitively price those items? Sure, but competitive pricing doesn't mean 10% under, or even level with, the nearest destination store. If yours is a convenience, regional competitor or niche store, your margins have to be higher to fuel your store's profitability.

At this point, I would be negligent if I didn't mention the old and tired points of "out-servicing" the big boys, of offering better-educated employees to assist in customer service. These points, as well as the shorter shopping times because of easier in-and-out convenience of some stores, contribute to customers' choices and are valid points of differentiation that buffer price variations.

But those points detract from the main point. That being that you must maintain safe-harbor balanced pricing. I challenge you to think of a way your store can serve your needs or the needs of its owner (if that is not you) if it does not produce adequate profit. Therefore, the burden of balancing price to accomplish this basic task rests solidly and solely on your shoulders.

Going back to the manager who defended his vendor's retail pricing system, I told him that the pricing that he was using in his store might have been a valid pricing strategy in some locations and in some stores. It was, however, not the right strategy for a product-driven niche store in this location. The use of a one-size-fits-all process was very counterproductive for his unique situation.

There is another point that I want to make. Within the lumber business there are several small jobbers across the country who still use paper catalogs. In other industries this is true as well. New catalog sheets arrive in the mail and the dealer or representative for the wholesale company changes those sheets out. The suggested retail prices in these books are simply devices to communicate dealer cost. In other words a retail price may reflect a 30% margin and so the retail price is

30 points above cost. However, many times the retail price is based on nothing more than simple multiplication. There was no supporting research to determine if the suggested price was a fair and reasonable, retail. Many dealers however view this suggested retail as the gospel of pricing and behave accordingly, either using it verbatim or worse yet discounting from it. Take the burden of pricing upon yourself and your store will benefit.

Another reoccuring phenomenon I have observed is that, after a few customer complaints about pricing, some managers will lower pricing. I disagree with this logic and I am not the only one.

In his book *Selling the Invisible* (one of my favorite books on marketing!), Harry Beckwith includes a chapter titled "Pricing: The Resistance Principle." In it he writes:

If no one complains about your price, it's too low.

If almost everyone complains, it's too high.

So if no price resistance is too low and 100% is too high, how much resistance is just right? How much resistance tells you that your price is right?

15% to 20%. And there is one simple reason why: Close to 10% of people will complain about any price. Some want a deal. Others are mistrustful and assume every price is overstated. Still others want to get the price they had in their mind when they apporached you, because it's the price they hoped for and already have budgeted in their mind.

So throw out the group that will object no matter what your price. Then ask: In the remaining cases, how often do I encounter resistance?

Resistance in 10% of those remaining cases — for a total of almost 20% — is about right. When it starts exceeding 25%, scale back. (13)

I agree with Mr. Beckwith and in fact there are a number of items in your store that you could raise prices on today that would cause no ill-effects on unit sales but would have a positive effect on your store's profitability.

This is not a new concept by any stretch of the imagination. In fact, we all know that there different levels of price sensitivity and that there are a number of elements that contribute to the sensitivity of an item. For example, items that are advertised regularly, used frequently, have a relative high price tag, or are project starters may be rather price sensitive.

My intention is not to make this a chapter about price sensitivity, but rather, to point out that you need to be cognizant of your store's slot and how it impacts your retails.

The store that I referred to earlier in this chapter was goaded into using low prices on many items because his vendor deemed them price sensitive. Whether those items were price sensitive is not the issue at all; the issue is that pricing was inadequate to maintain a workable margin range for this particular store slot. Couple that with the fact that his prices were below those of the local destination store, and it seems clear that this retailer's prices on the shopped items were just too low!

Perhaps it would help you to think of an invisible plate of glass hovering somewhere above a plane that represents your retail pricing. Glass has a certain and measurable amount of strength, and in my example, represents the upper limit of price acceptability to about 80% of our customers. Remember, the other 20% will complain no matter what, so let's discount their opinion.

A safe harbor pricing position, then, would be one that pressed firmly against that glass. Of course, we wouldn't want to push beyond it and shatter the barrier of perceived consumer acceptability, but it would benefit our store's profitability to be pressed right up against the glass. In other words, it would benefit you to test the upper limits of pricing. Remember Mr. Beckwith's contention that you should experience some resistance to your pricing and ask yourself, "How many complaints have I had on pricing today, this week, this month?"

Discovering the opportunity hidden in your current pricing structure takes some time and leg work. You should schedule time for reconnaissance on a weekly basis. Depending on the size of your operation, assign an appropriate number of employees to the task of shopping 30 or 40 items at a couple of your competitors' stores. Before you know it, you will have discovered areas of opportunity — probably some areas where you need to lower prices, as well. Through this discovery process, you will find ways to improve your store's profitability, which is again the primary reason for your store to exist. However, the bonus in this scenario is improving your store's price image.

Before you start the process, sit down with your store crew and discuss your store's differentiating characteristics. A word of caution, however: if your store is a destination store or a *price*-driven niche store, then price is a primary differentiating characteristic and you must be a price leader — there is very little room for deviance from this principle.

But if your store is a regional competitor, convenience, or a *product*-driven niche store, price is not your primary claim to fame. So you must ask yourself and your crew what the characteristics of your store are that bring in customers? The answer should include the things that I mentioned earlier, convenience, easy in-and-out shopping, better trained employees etc.

Now, for the really tough question! How much extra are people willing to pay for your store's differentiating qualities? I know, it's tough to answer, but it's of crucial importance. If you can not price at a level equal to the price leader and your store has no differentiating qualities, you are not in a safe harbor but instead, you are dead in the water. **Your store's total package must provide value for a consumer.**

When our company is working with clients, we go through a similar process. One of our main goals for this exercise is to educate all of the store employees to the fact that their store's goods are worth the price they are charging. If an employee sends a message to a customer that is contrary to this theme, that employee is a detriment to your goals. That is why this is one facet of staff communication that is vitally important.

After we have compiled price-shop information, we enter the data into a spreadsheet, which we designed to help us evaluate and adjust the retail pricing. We will position the study store within at least 8 points of the market average of two shopped competitors, and with a deviation no higher than 13 points above the market leader. There is no magic about these numbers, they can be changed as required, but this range allows us to press firmly against the glass barrier that I alluded to earlier.

We go through this evaluation with every item that was on our price-shop list. The store personnel are taught to use the system, and then they repeat the process over subsequent weeks and with different items. Over time, the store's pricing structure can be reinvented and, with diligent effort, its margins can improve — along with its pricing image.

As I mentioned you can set your store's tolerance ranges differently, of course, but the overall procedure is valid and the system is sound. If you would like to view a short flash movie that further illustrates the process that we use, or if you would like to download our spreadsheet, which makes the process easier, visit our website at www.discoverdbr. com.

Chapter 12: Points to Remember

1. Your store's retail prices must be both acceptable to consumers and adequate to produce fair and reasonable margins. This is "Safe-Harbor Balanced Pricing."
2. Vendor pricing systems can be a good starting point, but should not be misinterpreted to represent comprehensive systems. You must be cautious of allowing their systems to lull you into complacency.
3. Your store's profitability is ultimately your responsibility, not your vendor's.
4. Your store's slot should direct the way you position its retail prices.
5. Competitive pricing does not mean matching prices!

Chapter 12: Action Steps

1. Review industry reports to discover your industry's margin averages. Remember, these figures are just that, an average. Compare your store's current operating margin and determine your relative position.
2. Teach your store personnel about "value equations." Let them know that their ongoing self-improvement is part of the equation that allows your store to maintain a "safe-harbor balance" of retail pricing.
3. Relative to your store's size, assign an appropriate number of employees the responsibility of conducting weekly price-shops of 20-30 items at two of your store's competitors.
4. Download our Retail Pricing Optimizer at www.discoverdbr.com or write one of your own to guide you through the price adjustment procedure.
5. Share the process with your key personnel. Make them part of this very important procedure.

Discovery-Based Retail

Chapter 13

DISCOVERING: A VISION FOR THE FUTURE

There is an industry source, perhaps a trade organization, that regularly compiles data regarding profitability and other key indicators for most store types. Whatever your store offering, take time to find that information for your particular industry and use it.

The NRHA's "Cost of Doing Business Study" is one such report for the hardware and home center industry. This study, which is undertaken annually, provides valuable insight to dealers who participate as well as those who just use the information for reference. That said, however, I am surprised at how many managers don't take the time to study and benefit from it. It seems that this comparison between one's business and others in the industry should be a fundamental exercise for any informed operator.

I recently consulted with the owner of a mid-sized lumber/hardware operation. Using the data from the "Cost of Doing Business Study" we were able to identify many problem areas within the owner's operation. He was very surprised to learn that his payroll was well above industry averages while the productivity per employee, as you would suspect, was correspondingly low. Yes, he was as I said surprised, but not as surprised as I was to learn that he had never gone through this process himself.

Speaking of payroll, do you know how yours compares? For example, the 2005 NRHA survey reported that hardware stores in the $500,000 to $1 million volume range had average payroll expenses of 21.7% of sales. That percentage was broken down like this: Owners Payroll 5.4%; Other Employees 13.2%; Taxes 1.6%; Group Insurance 1.2%; and Benefit Plans 0.2%.

Does this mean that you should scramble to make your payroll mirror these percentages? Well, only if it means that you can cut everybody else's pay, give yourself a raise, and structure your new performance bonus by the end of the fiscal year. Just kidding!

My point is this: As you examine opportunities and if you consider cutting expense as one of those opportunities (you should), make sure that the expenses that you choose to cut are ones that should be cut. Cut fat, not muscle! A comparison against industry research can help you determine your best strategy. Perhaps *your* greatest opportunity lies in categories other than payroll.

The industry reports can also tell you if your margins are at average for your store type. Use that information along with your new knowledge regarding your store's slot to identify opportunity for improvement in this key category. Industry reports can give you clues over wide ranges of categories. These reference points are great guides, but what if we had reference points that served as destinations as well?

I was 14 years old when I got my first job. We lived on a farm, and Jess Parsons was our neighbor. One evening, Jess came over to ask me if I would like to learn how to drive a tractor and to help him with his spring plowing.

He said that he had already approved the plan with my parents, and so it was entirely up to me. I was excited, probably more about making a little spending money than the actual work that lay ahead. At any rate, I took the job and reported for work, and for my lessons, the next morning.

Jess taught me the basics of operating the old Farm-all tractor, I believe it was a Model M. After he had turned me loose to plow a few rows myself, he reviewed my work. I knew it wasn't great — to use an old saying, the rows were as crooked as a dog's hind leg.

To tell you the truth, I might have been satisfied if the rows were only as crooked as a dog's *front* leg, but I don't think Jess would've been. I didn't know how to do any better, though, how to plow any straighter.

And so Jess climbed up on the tractor, stood beside me, and explained that I needed to pick a point on the distant horizon. He pointed, indicating that maybe this tree or that tree or that old barn would make good visual anchors. He told me that, if I lined up one of those anchor points with the center of the tractor, and if I didn't take my eyes off of the anchor, I would magically start plowing straight rows because I would know where I was going.

It worked! On the next few passes, my rows were much straighter than any old dog's leg, front or hind, and I felt really good about doing the job right. Although it's been decades since he shared it with me, I have never forgotten Jess' lesson.

Jess passed away many years ago, and, if you talked to his daughter Myrna, she would probably rather tell the story of how I later drove that same tractor into the pond. However, I won't go in to that embarrassing tale in this book (you can ask me about it when me meet face-to-face one day).

What Jess taught me that warm spring day is a great metaphor for what I have tried to convey to you in this book. Perhaps the idea of assigning different values to so many attributes of your store's performance may, at first glance, seem over-the-top, but the various systems of measurement discussed in this book can be your visual anchors on the distant horizon. Each one, in a different way, can help you "plow straighter rows" in some facet of your store's operation. After performing the exercises included here, you'll have the benchmarks to measure your store's progress over time. You can set goals for a number of your store's attributes and by reaching for those goals, produce tangible differences in your store's profitability.

The University of St. Thomas uses the follwing chart labeled "Store and Product Life Cycle." You will see that it has a line drawn in the shape of a parabolic curve, rising in the center and falling on either end, although more gradually on the right than the left.

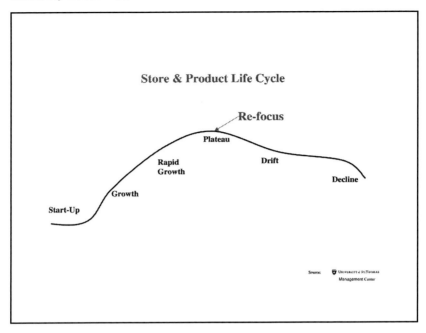

The left end is labeled "start up". The ascending arc on the left side of the curve is labeled "growth" and "rapid growth." The more slowly descending right-hand side of the curve comes after a short plateau area and is labeled "drift" and "decline." Notice that there is a boldfaced label that points to that top plateau area and reads simply "REFOCUS." Overall I like the chart, but perhaps we should take another lesson from it.

By now, you know that I like teaching with metaphors. So, hold on fans of the metaphorical, for here comes yet another one. Let's liken a store's life cycle represented in this chart to the flight of a rocket. It takes a tremendous amount of force and energy expenditure to get a rocket off the ground, but once in flight, it takes less thrust to continue it's upward travel if the controller applies more thrust while the rocket is still moving upward. Otherwise, once the rocket has started to lose altitude, it will have to fight inertia. Similarly, it takes less effort to overcome a retail operation's plateau if you start the push before you reach the plateau rather than after. In other words, a retail store should refocus its efforts regularly and not wait until the alarms have sounded.

Unfortunately, it's easy for store managers to get caught up in the mundane operational loops of everyday business and neglect the anchoring markers that are on the horizon.

Earlier in this book, I wrote that your store is either getting better or its getting worse, and that is exactly what the University of St. Thomas's "Store and Product Life Cycle" chart is pointing out to you.

As an aside, isn't it interesting that the chart suggests that a store's life cycle and a product's life cycle can be described in the same fashion? If you were to think of your store as being a product itself and not as just a location selling products, would you market it differently?

It's important to ask yourself what steps you've taken today that will make your store better next week or next month or next year. How will you keep your store on an ascending sales and profitability line? How will you avoid the plateau, let alone the drift and decline cycles?

The systems that I have outlined in this book can keep you on task in that regard, and its systems will help you define areas of opportunity for your business.

Now that you've read this book, there are several ways this story can be completed:

1. You may decide that you really didn't benefit that much from the time that you spent reading the book, and toss it in the circular file (obviously, I hope that doesn't happen).
2. You may decide that the book was interesting and informative and that maybe, one day, you'll think about some of the things that I suggested.
3. You may decide that you want to implement some of our systems today, put the book down, call your staff together, and begin making action plans to see that it happens.
4. You may decide you want to implement some of the changes suggested in the book but discover that you do not have the resources to do them yourself. You are invited to call our company or contact us at www.discoverdbr.com.

Obviously, I hope that you choose one of the last two options, and I sincerely hope that you enjoyed reading this book as much as I enjoyed writing it.

Please email your questions and comments to:
phil@discoverdbr.com

Bibliography

1. Wikipedia, "Demographic Gravitation" www.wikipedia.org
2. Spector, Robert "Category Killers": The retail revolution and its impact on consumer culture" Harvard Business School Press, 60 Harvard Way, Boston, MA. 02163
3. Collins, Jim "Good to Great, Why Some Companys Make the Leap...And Others Don't" HarperCollins Publishers, 10 East 53rd Street, New York, New York
4. Gladwell, Malcolm. "The Science of Shopping" New Yorker, November 4, 1996
5. Kaplan, Risa. www.bullmarket.com
6. The SoLux Company, www.soluxtli.com, Tailored Lighting, Inc., 50 Bermar Park, Suite 4A, Rochester, NY 14624
7. Wikipedia, www.wikipedia.org siting: Image of a "foot candle" distributed by General Electric during the 1960s as a promotional device. The "sole" of the candle (not shown) says "GE makes the difference in light!" This image originally appeared on eBay illustrating auction item #3300328026
8. 10022E Source Companies, 1965 North 57th Court, Boulder, Colorado 80301, USA 303-444-7788
9. As by M3 Planning, Inc. Powering MystrategicPlan.com
10. Wikipedia, www.wikipedia.org siting: Modell, Jack; Rosenthal NE, Harriett AE, Krishen A, Asgharian A, Foster VJ, Metz A, Rockett CB, Wightman DS (2005). "Seasonal affective disorder and its prevention by anticipatory treatment with bupropion XL Biological Psychiatry" 58 (8): 658-667.
11. Spector, Robert, "Category Killers: The retail revolution and its impact on consumer culture" Harvard Business School Press, 60 Harvard Way, Boston, MA. 02163
12. Scwartz, Barry, "The Paradox of Choice, Why More is Less", HarperCollins Publishers, 10 East 53rd Street, New York, New York, 10022
13. Beckwith, Harry "Selling the Invisible, A Field Guide to Modern Marketing", Warner Business Books, New York, New York

Index